ISLAMIC

ISLAMIC PHILOSOPHY AND THEOLOGY

W. MONTGOMERY WATT

EDINBURGH
at the University Press

EDINBURGH UNIVERSITY PRESS
22 George Square, Edinburgh

First Published 1962
Reprinted 1964, 1967, 1972
Paperback edition 1979
ISBN 0 85224 358 8

Printed in Great Britain by
The Scolar Press
Ilkley Yorks

FOREWORD

In 1939 the prospect of a war which would involve many Asian nations made men in positions of responsibility in Britain suddenly aware of the meagre number of our experts in Asian languages and cultures. The Scarbrough Commission was set up, and its report led to a great expansion of Oriental and African studies in Britain after the war. In the third decade after 1939 events are making clear to ever-widening circles of readers the need for something more than a superficial knowledge of non-European cultures. In particular the blossoming into independence of numerous African states, many of which are largely Muslim or have a Muslim head of state, emphasises the growing political importance of the Islamic world, and, as a result, the desirability of extending and deepening the understanding and appreciation of this great segment of mankind. Since history counts for much among Muslims, and what happened in 632 or 656 may still be a live issue, a journalistic familiarity with present conditions is not enough; there must also be some awareness of how the past has moulded the present.

This series of "Islamic surveys" is designed to give the educated reader something more than can be found in the usual popular books. Each work undertakes to survey a special part of the field, and to show the present stage of scholarship here. Where there is a clear picture this will be given; but where there are gaps, obscurities and differences of opinion, these will also be indicated. Full and annotated bibliographies will afford guidance to those who want to pursue their studies further. There will also be some account of the nature and extent of the source material.

will also be some account of the nature and extent of the source material.

While the series is addressed in the first place to the educated reader, with little or no previous knowledge of the subject, its character is such that it should be of value also to university students and others whose interest is of a more professional kind.

The transliteration of Arabic words is essentially that of the second edition of *The Encyclopaedia of Islam* (London, 1960, continuing) with three modifications. Two of these are normal with most British Arabists, namely, *q* for *ḳ*, and *j* for *dj*. The third is something of a novelty. It is the replacement of the ligature used to show when two consonants are to be sounded together by an apostrophe to show when they are to be sounded separately. This means that *dh*, *gh*, *kh*, *sh*, *th* (and in non-Arabic words *ch* and *zh*) are to be sounded together; where there is an apostrophe, as in *ad'ham*, they are to be sounded separately. The apostrophe in this usage represents no sound, but, since it only occurs between two consonants (of which the second is *h*), it cannot be confused with the apostrophe representing the glottal stop (*hamza*), which never occurs between two consonants.

W. Montgomery Watt
GENERAL EDITOR

CONTENTS

NOTE ON THE SOURCES

I PRIMARY MATERIAL

In this survey Islamic philosophy and theology are to be looked at together in a chronological framework. From a modern standpoint this juxtaposition of the two disciplines is important for the understanding of both; but it should be realized at the outset that it is a reversal of the traditional Islamic procedure. Not merely were the disciplines different, but in the earlier centuries the exponents were two different sets of persons, trained in two different educational traditions, each with its own separate institutions. There was little personal contact between philosophers and theologians, and the influence of the two disciplines on one another (chiefly of philosophy on theology) was largely by way of polemics. Eventually, as will be seen, while philosophy died out as a separate discipline, many parts of it were incorporated in theology; and it is noteworthy that the theologian chiefly responsible for this incorporation, al-Ghazālī (d. 1111), learned his philosophy not by attending lectures but by private reading. The relevance of this to a consideration of sources is that it must be kept in mind that two separate strands are being woven together.

The fundamental work for all Islamic source material in Arabic is Carl Brockelmann's *Geschichte der arabischen Literatur*, consisting of two original volumes (second edition, Leiden, 1943, 1949) and three supplementary volumes, (1937–42). This work lists all the manuscripts of Islamic Arabic works known to Western scholars up to the time of publication, as well as the printed editions. It also gives the dates of each author, where known, and a few biographical details, with references to notices in Arabic biographical dictionaries and to modern books and articles. The primary division is into chronological periods. In each period there are subdivisions according to subject, but each author appears only in one place. This means that not all the works on theology will appear under that heading ("Dogmatik"), since a man who was best known for Qur'ānic exegesis, and was placed under that heading, might also have written a work on theology. This invaluable compendium is commonly known as "Brockelmann" and referred to as *GAL* and *GALS*. For Christian Arabic literature (which includes some philosophy) it has to be supplemented by Georg GRAF's *Geschichte der christlichen arabischen Literatur* (Rome, Vatican, 1944–53), referred to as *GCAL*. This has similar information, but also contains readable introductions and full articles on the separate authors.

(a) *Philosophy*

For philosophy the primary sources are, of course, the works of the philosophers themselves. Unfortunately much of this material is not yet in a satisfactory condition for use by the historian of philosophy. Carefully edited modern texts of the chief works of the great philosophers are gradually becoming available, notably those by Maurice BOUYGES in the *Bibliotheca Arabica Scholasticorum* (Catholic Press, Beirut), but in many cases much work still requires to be done on the actual text. Besides the accidents to which a text in any language was liable when manuscripts were copied by scribes, there are some peculiar to Arabic. Owing to the absence of vowels in normal Arabic writing, there are more possible ways of taking words and phrases wrongly if one is not following the argument; and the flexibility of Arabic makes it hard sometimes to detect false letters and words which have crept into the text, since there is usually some way of taking them that *nearly* makes sense.

Another unsatisfactory feature of the material is that extant manuscripts contain a large number of small and minor works or fragments of works. Sometimes there is no title, or the title may vary in different manuscripts, or different works may have the same title. There is often doubt about the ascription to an author which is given in the manuscripts, or works may appear without any author's name. Altogether there is a vast tangle of problems about the identity and authorship of many works, and this tangle can only be unravelled by a vast amount of patient scholarly work.

The consequence of these features of the material is that anyone who writes about Islamic philosophy and philosophers in a general way is taking a large risk. All kinds of things may happen which make his wider statements false. The text of a crucial passage may be proved to be erroneous; a new work by the author in question may be discovered; or a work supposed to be his may be shown to be by someone else. Thus most of the general statements about Islamic philosophy made at the present time must be regarded as in part provisional. The scholar, then, who would write about Islamic philosophy is in a dilemma. If he is very careful, he will hesitate to say anything at all. If he is concerned to try to meet the world's desire to know a little about Islamic philosophy, he will give some account, while knowing that what he says is based on inferior editions and does not refer to all the relevant passages. What is said below about Islamic philosophy is naturally open to criticism of this kind.

(b) *Theology*

The material for theology, though not immune to the defects of the philosophical material, is in much better condition. There are still textual errors to be spotted and remedied, but there is much greater certainty about the major works of the chief theologians. The earliest extant works of Sunnite theology in the strict sense are those of al-Ashʿarī (d. 935), but theological doctrines are stated or implied in earlier works on law, tradition and mysticism. From this time onwards innumerable works were written, including some of the type of a Summa Theologica and shorter essays on particular subjects. Those translated into European languages will be mentioned in the separate chapters. Qur'ānic commentaries normally have a specific theological standpoint, which influences the interpretation of some verses, and frequently contain expositions of points of theology.

Credal statements or, for simplicity, "creeds" also exist in considerable numbers, and some are earlier in date than the first theological works. Their function is different from that of the creeds of Christendom. They were not official formulations of the doctrinal beliefs of the main body of believers, but merely statements of the tenets of particular theologians or schools. The earlier instances are brief, but some of the later ones are lengthy, so that it is difficult to draw a firm line between the creed and the theological treatise. Like many other branches of Arabic literature they had extensive commentaries written on them. They are sometimes included in comprehensive works on jurisprudence, since it was a "legal" obligation (according to the Sharīʿa) to believe certain doctrines and profess them publicly.

II SECONDARY MATERIAL

(a) *Heresiography*

Since the earliest works of theology proper in Islam were not written until about 900, we have to look elsewhere for material about the early formative period. One important class of material is that about the heretical sects and sectaries which is conveniently called "heresiography". The main general heresiographies are those of al-Ash'arī (d. 935), al-Baghdādī ('Abd-al-Qāhir ibn-Ṭāhir) (d. 1037), ash-Shahrastānī (d. 1153) and Ibn-Ḥazm (d. 1064). There are also partial heresiographies such as *The Sects of the Shī'a* usually ascribed to an-Nawbakhtī (d. *c.* 910).[1] Many works dealing with theology or even history have chapters on the sects, and some of these contain valuable material not in the general heresiographies.

A more careful study of the formation of the heresiographical tradition is a desideratum for extending our knowledge of the development of theology before 900. It has long been recognized that some of the heresiographers arranged their works to accord with a Tradition that there were seventy-three sects in Muḥammad's community;[2] they achieved their end by counting as separate sects groups of people whose views differed only slightly from one another.

This only affects the arrangement of the works, however; and the nature of the information itself needs to be more closely scrutinized. Modern scholars until very recently have tended to assume that the heresiographers wrote from a neutral viewpoint and that the information they gave was mostly quite objective. A little reflection, however, shows the danger of this assumption. Thus al-Ash'arī sometimes mentions his sources, and some of the people he mentions possibly wrote short and partial heresiographies. It seems certain, however, that both al-Ashʿarī and his sources obtained information from polemical works in which the writer mentioned the views of various persons and then refuted them. One such work from the later ninth century is extant, *Le Livre de triomphe* (*Kitāb al-Intiṣār*) by al-Khayyāṭ (edited by H. S. Nyberg, Cairo, 1925; French translation by A. Nader, 1957). Now books like this cannot be expected to give impartial accounts of men's views. Indeed, the book mentioned illustrates this, for al-Khayyāṭ is a Muʿtazilite and most of his book is spent in accusing his opponent, a renegade from the Muʿtazilites, of having misrepresented the views of earlier members of this sect.

This point becomes more serious when we look at the list of early heresiographers compiled by Hellmut RITTER ("Philologika III: Muhammedanische Häresiographen", *Der Islam*, xviii [1929], 34-55). Apart from some of the writers about the Shīʿites most of these sources of information are Muʿtazilite or Ashʿarite. The first three general heresiographies mentioned above are Ashʿarite; and the Ashʿarites are the school founded by al-Ashʿarī who was originally a Muʿtazilite. In other words, our main heresiographical tradition is Muʿtazilite and Ashʿarite; and these are really two strands of a single tradition.

Recent studies, however, of the Ḥanbalites inaugurated by Henri LAOUST are showing that there is a Ḥanbalite heresiographical tradition distinct from the main one. There is also a somewhat rudimentary Khārijite tradition, which has been studied above all at the Oriental Institute in Naples; it refers mainly to the earliest period. One curious discrepancy is that a sect called the Jahmites which is prominent in the Ḥanbalite tradition receives only slight mention in the Muʿtazilite-Ashʿarite tradition. The explanation appears to be that for the Ḥanbalites the connotation of the name was much wider than for the Muʿtazilites and indeed included the latter. This is also an example of another fact which has to be kept in mind. Some of the names of sects are nicknames given by opponents and not accepted by the sect or group in question. Thus the name "Qadarite" in the main heresiographers means a believer in human freedom (as contrasted with divine omnipotence); but at an early stage in the discussions on the question the upholders of free will tried to fasten the name "Qadarite" on their opponents who believed in God's *qadar*, that is, determination of all events including human acts. No one ever seems to have called himself a Qadarite. Even in the standard usage the name refers to a doctrinal tendency rather than membership of a particular group of theologians; in this it would be comparable to some of our modern terms such as "fundamentalist", "evangelical", "high-church".[3]

(b) *Biography and History*

One of the features of Arabic literature is the interest in biography. This is perhaps connected with the Arab conception of knowledge as something which is transmitted by the transmission of a form of words. It is then important to know whether the transmitters were reliable persons, and so to know something about their lives. The outstanding instance of this emphasis on biography is in the case of the Traditions (that is, the anecdotes about things Muḥammad had said or done, which were used to justify legal and liturgical practice—in this technical sense the word is here spelt with a capital).[4] Besides the biographies of Traditionists there are also specialized biographical dictionaries dealing with the members of particular theological or legal schools and often arranged according to "generations" (*ṭabaqāt*); e.g. of Shāfiʿites, Ḥanafites, Ḥanbalites, Ashʿarites, Muʿtazilites, ṣūfīs (mystics). The biographical notices do not always contain the information we might expect, but they mostly have a list of the man's teachers and pupils, and thus demonstrate the continuity in the teaching of the particular school. The philosophers, as noted above, belonged to a distinct educational tradition, and their biographical notices occur in dictionaries which also comprise notices of astronomers, physicians and other representatives of Greek learning (and including Aristotle, Galen and other Greeks in the same list as the much later Islamic scholars). Some of the theologians and philosophers are mentioned in a comprehensive *Biographical Dictionary*, mainly of literary figures, by IBN-KHALLIKĀN (d. 1282), translated into English by Baron MacGuckin de Slane.[5]

Biographical notices are also included in many historical works. One that may be mentioned, since it has been translated into French, is *The Golden Meadows* by AL-MASʿŪDI (d. 956).[6] In so far as theologians took part in political events they are naturally mentioned in general histories; this fact is relevant in the case of risings or revolts for which a theological justification was given, such as those of the Khārijites and Shīʿites. Useful information about early philosophers and sectaries is contained in an unusual book, the *Fihrist* or *Index* of AN-NADĪM (composed in 988); this is a vast list of all the books known to the author, who was probably a bookseller, together with a few biographical notes.

BIBLIOGRAPHY

For ash-Shahrastānī see next section.

AL-BAGHDĀDĪ, *Al-Farq bayn al-Firaq*—an English translation of the second half, *Moslem Schisms and Sects, Part II*, by Abraham S. Halkin (Tel-Aviv, 1935), is accurate and has much useful information in the notes. A translation of the first half by Kate C. Seeley was published in New York in 1919, but withdrawn because of numerous faults.

III MODERN STUDIES

(a) *The beginnings*

About the twelfth century knowledge of Islamic philosophy reached Europe through Spain, and led to the movement of Latin Averroism and the reaction of Thomism. Apart from this no attention was paid in Europe to either Islamic theology or philosophy until the nineteenth century. The doctrinal aspects of Islam were indeed known in some detail, as can be seen from the "Preliminary Discourse" of the still valuable translation of the Qur'ān made by George SALE in 1734; but this knowledge was at a popular rather than a theological level, and was based not on theological works, but mainly on the Qur'ān. The first theological work to be studied appears to be the Creed of the Ottoman theologian Birgevi (d. 1573), which was translated from Turkish by J. H. GARCIN DE TASSY in his *Exposition de la foi musulmane* (Paris, 1822). Knowledge of the Islamic sects was greatly increased by William CURETON's edition of the heresiography of ash-Shahrastānī (London, 1842–46) and its subsequent translation into German by T. HAARBRÜCKER (Halle, 1850–51). The first careful study of philosophy was by August SCHMÖLDERS who published texts and an essay in 1836 and 1842. A little later came Salomon MUNK's *Mélanges de philosophie juive et arabe* (Paris, 1859), and on the theological side Alfred VON KREMER's *Geschichte der herrschenden Ideen des Islams* (Leipzig, 1868); both of these have been considered worth republishing by a photographic method. So also has been Moritz STEINSCHNEIDER's *Die arabischen Übersetzungen aus dem*

Griechischen (Graz, 1960), which originally appeared in different journals from 1889 to 1896, and contains material indispensable for an understanding of the beginnings of Islamic philosophy. By the painstaking labours of these and other scholars, in cataloguing manuscripts, forming a general idea of their contents and publishing some of the most important, the foundations were being laid.

(b) *Theology*

Towards the end of the nineteenth century, too, Muslim scholars in Egypt and elsewhere were publishing medieval books, and Islamic theology in particular benefited from this. These editions were uncritical and usually based on a single manuscript, but nevertheless facilitated an extension of the knowledge of Islamic theology among Western students. The outstanding figure in this sphere is Ignaz GOLDZIHER, of Hungarian Jewish descent, and professor in Budapest. The width of his reading is astounding, especially when one considers that he had few printed editions and no microfilms, and had to travel to many libraries to consult the manuscripts he needed. With this reading he combined a sureness of judgement, and his many articles in learned journals on theological subjects are still nearly all of the highest importance. He did not of course confine himself to theology, but wrote on many aspects of Islamic religion and also on philosophy and law, so that with good reason he is generally regarded as the founder of the modern scholarly discipline of Islamic studies. His mature conceptions on theology and connected matters are contained in his lectures on Islam (*Vorlesungen über den Islam*), originally composed about 1908 and revised for a second edition (Heidelberg, 1925). His lectures on Qur'ānic exegesis (*Die Richtungen der islamischen Koranauslegung*, Leiden, 1920) are also relevant.

Another pioneer is Duncan Black MACDONALD, born on the west coast of Scotland, and professor at Hartford Seminary, Connecticut. He was a scholar of sound judgement, though he had not the depth of reading of Goldziher, and he wrote many of the theological articles in the first edition of *The Encyclopaedia of Islam* (Leiden, 1913–42), of which he was also an editor. The section on theology (pp. 119-287, with the appendix, pp. 291-357) of his book on the *Development of Muslim Theology, Jurisprudence and Constitutional Theory* (New York, 1903), though now out-of-date in parts, is still the best introductory account in English.

A work whose title does not indicate its importance for Islamic theology is *La Passion . . . d'al-Hallaj, martyr mystique de l'Islam* (d. 922) by Louis MASSIGNON (Paris, 1922); chapter 12 (pp. 535-771) deals with dogmatic theology, comparing al-Ḥallāj with his predecessors and contemporaries, and containing so much information succinctly expressed that the would-be reader is soon discouraged. Nevertheless this book cannot be neglected by the serious student, nor indeed can the same author's *Essai sur les origines du Lexique technique de la mystique musulmane* (second edition, Paris, 1954). In general it may be remarked that most studies of sufism (or Islamic mysticism) touch on the fringes of theology, but such works will not be dealt with here.[7]

Another book which must be mentioned is *The Muslim Creed*, by the Dutch scholar, Arent Jan WENSINCK (Cambridge, 1932). This is a study of the growth of the dominant Sunnite dogmatic position, based on the author's wide knowledge of the Traditions. A slight weakness is his failure to distinguish various strands within Sunnism, especially the Ḥanafite (or Māturīdite), from which most of the creeds studied are taken, and the Ashʿarite.

The most serious attempt to survey the wide range of theological works now available in print and to look at the development of theology as a whole is that of Louis GARDET and M. M. ANAWATI (the latter an Arab Dominican). Their *Introduction à la théologie musulmane* (Paris, 1948) marked a great step forward, and two further volumes are promised dealing with particular doctrines in detail. The one criticism which might be made is that the Thomistic standpoint of the authors makes them treat their subject in a way that may be strange to readers who do not share this standpoint.

Apart from the works discussed above and those mentioned in bibliographies below, there is now little value in anything on Islamic theology written before 1914.

(c) *Philosophy*

The study of Islamic philosophy has progressed more slowly than that of theology. Although it had commenced before the middle of the nineteenth century, it cannot yet be said to have reached the level of attainment of the study of theology under Macdonald and Goldziher. This is largely due to the much less satisfactory condition of the texts. Muslim scholars, too, until the last decade or two, have been less inclined to publish texts, since for them the philosophers ranked as heretics. Such advances as have been made have been due to the laborious editing of texts by Western scholars, notably Friedrich DIETERICI (*floruit* 1865-1890) and Maurice BOUYGES (*floruit* 1920–1945), a Jesuit and founder of the Bibliotheca Arabica Scholasticorum. Much had been achieved by way of discovering texts by Paul KRAUS before his early death in 1945. Several Western scholars are now working in this field, and some useful contributions have been made by the Egyptian ʻAbd-ar-Raḥmān BADAWĪ.

A consequence of the inadequacy of the texts is that

there is no satisfactory account of Islamic philosophy as a whole. The most balanced is that of the Dutchman Tjitje DE BOER, originally published in German in 1901, and subsequently in an English translation as *The History of Philosophy in Islam* (London, 1903). The basic facts are presented with tolerable accuracy, though some statements require to be modified in the light of later discoveries. The kind of modification required will be seen from the chapter on "Islamic Philosophy" by Richard WALZER in *History of Philosophy, Eastern and Western*, edited by S. Radhakrishnan (London, 1953), II. 120-48; also in his *Greek into Arabic*, 1-28.

Less satisfactory are the general accounts of Islamic philosophy by Max HORTEN and Goffredo QUADRI (in both Italian and French).[8] Horten did much work on Islamic philosophy and philosophical theology between about 1905 and 1920, but he has been generally adjudged not wholly reliable. Profit is still to be had from his writings, however, by the careful student who is prepared to work with the sources in conjunction with his reading of Horten. Quadri tends to regard earlier Islamic philosophy as a preparation for Averroes, and thus sees the whole development from an unsatisfactory perspective.

The bibliography of European works on Islamic philosophy by the Dominican Pierre Jean DE MENASCE —*Bibliographische Einführungen in das Studium der Philosophie: 6, Arabische Philosophie* (Bern, 1948), is to be thoroughly recommended.

BIBLIOGRAPHY

Gustav PFANNMÜLLER, *Handbuch der Islam-Literatur* (Berlin and Leipzig, 1923); a valuable bibliography and description of Islamic studies in Europe up to the time of publication.

J. D. PEARSON, *Index Islamicus, 1906–55* (Cambridge, 1958); a classified and exhaustive list of articles in learned journals dealing with Islamic subjects; supplements are promised to bring it up to date. The sections specially relevant to theology and philosophy are: II; IV, a, b.

A. S. TRITTON, *Muslim Theology* (London, 1948), a survey of the earlier period, mainly devoted to sectaries, each being treated separately; rather detailed for the general reader, but has some useful references.

W. MONTGOMERY WATT, *Free Will and Predestination in Early Islam* (London, 1948); studies this topic in writers up to 950, especially the Muʿtazilites and al-Ashʿarī.

W. MONTGOMERY WATT, *Islam and the Integration of Society* (London, 1961); chapters 7 and 8 are relevant.

J. WINROW SWEETMAN, *Islam and Christian Theology* (London, 1945, 1947, 1955, continuing); a collection of information covering a wide field, though not leading to any conclusions in its incomplete state.

Dwight M. DONALDSON, *Studies in Muslim Ethics* (London, 1953); has chapters on the ethics of philosophers and theologians. The article by H. A. R. GIBB and R. WALZER in *EI*² on "Akhlāḳ" (Ethics) is good.

Sir Thomas ARNOLD and Alfred GUILLAUME, *The Legacy of Islam* (Oxford, 1931), pp. 239-83, "Philosophy and Theology" (by A. Guillaume); chiefly concerned with the influence of Islamic thought on Europe and its transmission through Spain.

De Lacy O'LEARY, *Arabic Thought and its Place in History*, London, 1922; the best parts of this book are those dealing with the transmission of philosophical thought from Greek through Syriac to Arabic, and then, sometimes through Hebrew, to Latin; it is being rapidly superseded.

Hermann STIEGLECKER, *Die Glaubenslehren des*

Islam, Munich, 1959, continuing; an ambitious attempt to present Islamic belief as it appears to Muslims, but based on somewhat dubious presuppositions and giving no detailed references.

The Encylopædia of Islam: first edition, four vols. and supplement, Leiden, 1913–42; second edition, vol. 1, Leiden and London, 1960, continuing. Articles dealing with religion from the first edition, but often with some revision, were published in a separate volume as *Handwörterbuch des Islam* (1941) and *A Shorter Encyclopaedia of Islam* (1953). The worth of the articles naturally varies; some of the older ones in the first edition are now unsatisfactory. Many are extremely important, however, since they are based on oriental sources, and contain material not otherwise accessible in European languages. Abbreviations: *EI*[1], *EI*[2], *EI(S)*.

A. J. Arberry, *Revelation and Reason in Islam*, London, 1957; general review with references to recently published texts.

Part One

THE UMAYYAD PERIOD

CHAPTER I

THE BEGINNINGS OF SECTARIANISM

BETWEEN Muḥammad's migration to Medina in 622 and his death in 632 he was able to build up a state of considerable power. A measure of the size of the state is that on an expedition towards Syria at the end of 630 Muḥammad had 30,000 men behind him. Many, perhaps most, of the nomadic tribes of Arabia were in alliance with him, the chief exceptions being those in the Byzantine sphere of influence. The immediately following period, from 632 to 661, is known as that of the "rightly-guided caliphs". Abū-Bakr (632–4) was mostly occupied in quelling the revolt of certain tribes against the Medinan political system. Under ʿUmar I (634–44) a phenomenal expansion took place; Syria and Egypt were wrested from the Byzantine empire and Iraq from the Persian. For the first half of the reign of ʿUthmān (644–56) expansion continued into North Africa and Persia; but about 650 it slowed down, discontent appeared among the troops (who were identical with the citizen body), and in 656 ʿUthmān was killed by mutineers. ʿAlī, the cousin and son-in-law of Muḥammad, was then acclaimed as caliph in Medina, but Muʿāwiya, governor of Damascus, among others, refused to recognize him. In the struggle between ʿAlī and Muʿāwiya the latter was slowly gaining the upper hand when in 661 ʿAlī was murdered for a private grievance. Muʿawiya's caliphate was then generally recognized, and the Umayyad dynasty thereby established.

This recital of historical events is not irrelevant to our theological concern. Exponents of the sociology of knowledge would hold that all theological and philosophical ideas have a political or social reference; and the standpoint of this survey is in accordance with such an outlook. The connection between theology and politics is particularly close and obvious in the Middle East. The Old Testament is full of it. In the early seventh century the disaffection of the native Christians of Syria and Egypt to the Byzantine emperor found a focus in the Monophysite and Nestorian heresies. It is therefore not surprising that in the discussions in chapters 1–3 it will be difficult to say what is politics and what theology. Nevertheless, apart from the "false prophets" who inspired the revolts, known as the Ridda or "apostasy", from about 632 to 634, no theological element is discernible in the political conflicts within the Islamic state until just before the beginning of the Umayyad period. This was not due, either, to the absence of strife and tension. The rivalry between the two main tribes of Medina continued almost to the time of Muḥammad's death; in the appointment of a successor the jealousy of the Medinans towards the Meccans came to light; in the wars of "apostasy" certain nomadic tribes were opposing the Medinans, Meccans and certain other nomadic tribes; and the accession of ʿAlī brought into the open a clash of interests between at least three different groups of Meccans.

A theological factor first comes into contact with politics in certain disputes which took place among the followers of ʿAlī. These were mostly men from nomadic tribes, now settled in military camp-towns in Iraq; and the disputes occurred when ʿAlī, after defeating one group of Meccan opponents in a battle near Basra, was trying to collect a sufficient army to meet his more serious rival, Muʿāwiya, who had at his disposal the army occupying Syria. Among the troops under ʿAlī's command were some who were deeply attached to him; they are said to have sworn that they would be "friends of those whom he befriended and enemies of those to whom he was hostile". In other words, these men believed that a leader or imām such as ʿAlī could make no mistakes and do no wrong. The opposing group not merely thought that ʿAlī was capable of making mistakes, but regarded him as actually in error because he was not sufficiently definite in his support of those responsible for the murder of ʿUthmān. This second group considered themselves in a sense the spiritual descendants of the men who had killed ʿUthmān (though there does not appear to have been much personal continuity). ʿUthmān, they held, had sinned in that he had not punished the crime of a prominent member of his administration; and by this sin he had forfeited the privileges that went with membership of the community, thereby rendering it not merely no sin but even a duty for Muslims to kill him.

There were probably many men in ʿAlī's army whose views came somewhere between these extremes; but it is the extremes that are important for the later theological developments. The two groups described are in fact the beginnings of the two great sects of the Shīʿites and the Khārijites. The Shīʿites derive their name from the fact that they are *par excellence* the "party" (*shīʿa*), that is, of ʿAlī. The Khārijites (in Arabic usually Khawārij, singular Khārijī) were so called because they "went out" or "seceded" (*kharajū*), first from ʿAlī and then from Muʿāwiya and the Umayyads. The best-known instances of such "secessions" are two which occurred while ʿAlī was getting ready to march against the army of Syria. The first party, who went to a place called Ḥarūrāʾ, returned when ʿAlī met some of their grievances; but some of the second party refused to be reconciled and were eventually massacred. The frequency with which the story of these events is repeated should not be allowed to obscure the fact that there were five other small risings against ʿAlī and about twenty during the reign of Muʿāwiya (661–80). There were also, of course, several more serious Khārijite risings at various times during the Umayyad period, and some historians have suggested that "Khārijite" simply means "rebel"; but a study of the theological side of the movement will show that this is not so.

The occurrence of risings under both ʿAlī and Muʿāwiya proves that they were not due to personal dislike of the rule of either man, but must have resulted from some general features of the situation. Reflection suggests what these features were. The men concerned in the Khārijite risings were not of Meccan or Medinan origin, but men from nomadic tribes. Thirty years earlier these men and their fathers had been living the free life of the desert. Now they were caught up into the vast organization of the Muslim army. When the campaigns were over, they went back not to the familiar desert but to camp-cities in Iraq or Egypt. At this early period all Muslims were expected to take part in military service, and in return they received a stipend from the state. The amount of the stipend varied according to the priority of the family in adhesion to Islam. Though there is scope here for many economic grievances, there do not appear from the records to have been any such. It therefore seems probable that the underlying reason for the risings was the general sense of *malaise* and insecurity consequent on the rapid and abrupt changes. It is further probable that the incipient Shīʿite movement is a different response to the same sense of *malaise* and insecurity.

This hypothesis makes possible an explanation both of the different responses to the situation of the Shīʿites and the Khārijites, and also of the intense hostility between them. In a time of change, insecurity and crisis men tend to look for salvation to the thing in their past experience that has proved most fundamental and satisfying (whether they are fully conscious of what they are doing or not). It appears to be a fact that some men believe that salvation (or the attainment of the supreme end of human life) is to be found in the following of a leader who is endowed with more than human qualities. Such qualities are usually believed to be the gift of a god, though occasionally they may be thought of rather as a natural endowment. It is convenient to use the sociological term "charismata" and to speak of a "charismatic leader". It also appears to be a fact that other men look for salvation not to a leader but to a community possessing certain charismata. By being a member of such a community (and by doing nothing to forfeit one's membership) a man attains salvation. The negative form of this belief occurs in the tag: *extra ecclesia nulla salus*. The positive aspect was prominent in the thought of many Muslims, for they spoke of the Islamic community as "the people of Paradise", implying that all the members would eventually attain to Paradise.

The existence of deep-seated beliefs of this kind explains the appearance of the Khārijite and Shī'ite movements during the caliphate of 'Alī. In the stresses and strains of the completely new life into which they had been plunged, men were in need of something firm and secure. Deep, probably unconscious, impulses made them seek this security, some by following a leader with the charisma of infallibility, others by trying to ensure that the community of which they were members was a charismatic one. For the first group the old Arab belief that special qualities of character were handed down in certain families justified them in taking 'Alī as a leader of infallible wisdom, even when his actual political decisions were hardly in accordance with this belief. The second group had a certain advantage in that the community of Muslims had undoubtedly been founded by a divinely inspired prophet and possessed a way of life supernaturally revealed to it; to ensure that this community remained the people of Paradise, however, it was necessary, some of them felt, that those who broke the rules should be excluded from it. In this way there arose the distinctive Khārijite tenet that those who have committed a grave sin are thereby excluded from the community. Positively the Khārijites were seeking security in the knowledge that the community to which they belonged was a supernatural or charismatic one.

Further reflection along these lines shows why there was such bitterness between Khārijites and Shīʿites. For both groups the question was one of whether they were going to attain salvation or realize their supreme end; one might say roughly that it was a matter of life and death. In this situation the beliefs of each group contradicted those of the other; and so each group was in the position of preventing the other from attaining salvation. The Khārijites, not convinced of the infallibility of the leader, saw rather that he might make a mistake and thereby lead the whole community into a course of action which would cause them to forfeit their status as people of Paradise. The Shīʿites, on the other hand, were horrified at the prospect that ordinary uninspired members of the community might, by their interpretation of its scriptures (which the Shīʿites did not regard as infallible), cause the inspired leader to adopt a course of action which he knew to be wrong. In this way each group's chance of salvation, as they saw it, was endangered by the other group. It is not surprising that there was bitter hostility between them.

What has been said so far is fairly well established. When it comes, however, to the question why some men should turn to the charismatic leader and others to the charismatic community, there is an explanation that can be given, but for the moment it must be regarded as a hypothesis needing further examination (chiefly by comparing parallel instances in other cultures). It is conceivable that the two reactions to the same situation are due to ultimate and fundamental differences in the human constitution; but this is a dubious theory with serious consequences, and so it is preferable, if it can be done, to explain the differences by hereditary or environmental factors. There are two points which help towards an explanation.

The first point is that there are resemblances between the little groups of Khārijite rebels and the effective units of nomadic society. In the risings during the reigns of ʿAlī and Muʿāwiya we are usually told the number of men involved, and it varies between thirty and five hundred, with an average of about two hundred. They did not retire to the desert, so far as we can judge, but merely withdrew to a safe distance from the towns of Iraq, and presumably kept themselves alive by raiding or by levying food from the countryside, until a government force suppressed them. Each little band presumably regarded itself as the core of the community of genuine Muslims, though not denying that there were genuine Muslims apart from the band. Most other men, however, were not genuine Muslims and therefore could be killed with impunity. Thus in various ways the little revolting bands were creating a form of life not unlike that of the divisions of a nomadic tribe. It was not exactly regression to desert conditions, for the basis of the Khārijite group was religion and not kinship. Yet it is significant that the Khārijites, like the nomads in earlier days, became noted for their skill as poets and orators; and, despite their Islamic faith, the sentiments expressed in their poems are close to those of the pagan nomads.

The second point to be noted is that, when one asks to which tribes the early Shīʿites and Khārijites belonged, a definite difference is found. The difference is not absolute, for a great many tribes are mentioned on both sides; but what can be asserted is that (1) a significant proportion of the early Shīʿites came from the tribes of South Arabia, and (2) the doctrinally important individuals and sects among the Khārijites (during the Umayyad period as a whole) were mainly from three northern tribes. Moreover, there does not seem to be anything in the history of the period from 622 to 656 to explain this difference of reaction. The northern tribes as a whole had been earlier in joining the Muslim raids into Iraq; but at least one tribe prominent among the Shīʿites had shared in the early raids. ʿAlī had been sent by Muḥammad to perform special duties in South Arabia, but there is no mention of his gaining the special affection of the people. Whether the environments from which the members of these tribes came had been deeply influenced by Judaism or Monophysite or Nestorian Christianity is a point that could be further investigated; but, even if some such influence can be proved, it does not look like giving the whole explanation.

The hypothesis to be put forward is that the difference in reaction is due to century-old traditions. The South Arabian tribes stood somehow within the tradition of the ancient civilization of that region, more than a thousand years old. In this civilization there had been divine or semi-divine kings. Even if the Arab tribesmen of the seventh century had not themselves lived under kings, they must unconsciously have been affected by the tradition, within which it had been usual in times of danger to rely on the superhuman leadership of the king. Because of this they in their time of crisis looked about for a leader of this type, and thought they had found one in ʿAlī. The members of the northern tribes had not been within the sphere of influence of the belief in divine kingship. On the contrary, the normal practice in the desert tribes was for all the adult males to be regarded as in certain respects equal; and there are traces of "democratic communities" of this kind far back in the pre-history of Iraq. Along with this practice of equality went a belief that outstanding excellence belonged to the tribe and the tribal stock, so that merely to have the blood of the tribe in one's veins gave one a place of honour in the world. The Arabs of the time just before Muḥammad gave this belief a this-worldly interpretation; but in the crisis round about 656 it would not be surprising if the idea of a small community of genuine Muslims evoked a deep unconscious response from those who had lived in this "democratic" tradition. This at least is the view that is here propounded as a hypothesis.

Bibliography

The views expressed here are formulated with greater detail in my previous writings: "Shīʿism under the Umayyads", *Journal of the Royal Asiatic Society*, 1960, 158-72; "Khārijite Thought in the Umayyad Period", *Der Islam*, xxxvi (1961), 215-31; "The Conception of the Charismatic Community in Islam", *Numen*, vii (1960), 77-90; *Islam and the Integration of Society*, 94-114. These are also relevant to the next two chapters.

M. G. S. Hodgson, art. "ʿAbd Allāh b. Sabaʾ" in *EI²*.

CHAPTER 2

THE KHĀRIJITES

MUʿĀWIYA reigned as universally recognized caliph from 661 to 680. His power rested chiefly on the army composed of the Arabs settled in Syria, and he made Damascus his capital. In the practice of the nomadic Arabs a chief was usually succeeded by the best qualified member of his family; primogeniture and even sonship gave no special rights. This gave little guidance in arranging for the succession to the caliphate. Muʿāwiya tried to have his son Yazīd acknowledged as successor before his own death, but even so there were some who did not accept Yazīd. The opposition led to a catastrophic civil war when Yazīd died in 683, leaving only a minor son. ʿAbd-Allāh ibn-az-Zubayr (or, more simply, Ibn-az-Zubayr), who had defied Yazīd from Mecca, now gained control of much of Iraq as well as of the region of Mecca and Medina. There was widespread confusion, and vast tracts of the caliphate were under the effective control of neither the Umayyads nor Ibn-az-Zubayr. Under the leadership of a member of another branch of the family the Umayyads fought back; in 691 they completed the recovery of Iraq, and before the end of 692 extinguished the last flames of revolt in Mecca.

The expansion of the caliphate, which had continued under Muʿāwiya but had been stopped by the civil war, was now resumed. In the east the Muslims extended their sway to Central Asia and north-west India; while in north Africa they pressed westwards into Morocco, and in 711 crossed the straits into Spain. To the north there were frequent expeditions against the Byzantines, but no permanent occupation of territory proved possible. The vastness of the territories ruled led to ever-increasing internal tensions, and the clumsy administrative machine lumbered along with creaks and groans. From about 730 or 735 it must have been clear to acute observers that the empire was slowly breaking up, and some of these observers attempted, by staging a revolt, to create an alternative government. None was successful, however, though they played a part in weakening the Umayyads, until eventually in 750 the armies of the ʿAbbāsid movement from the east swept into Iraq, liquidated the Umayyad regime, and established the new dynasty of the ʿAbbāsids.

Two Khārijite movements which greatly stimulated theological development sprang up and grew to a considerable size during the civil war of Ibn-az-Zubayr. The first of these is the sub-sect of the AZRAQITES (Azāriqa), so named from their original leader, Nāfiʿ ibn-al-Azraq. Some of the Khārijites from Basra had sympathized with Ibn-az-Zubayr (as an opponent of the Umayyads) and had given him active help. In time, however, they seem to have realized that, even if successful, he would not rule according to their ideas. When Basra went over to him in 684, the Azraqites took to the mountains eastwards. Though their leader was killed in the following year, they were able to increase and maintain their strength, so that for a time (about 691) they were a threat to Basra. After the end of the civil war the Umayyad armies were able to exterminate them (but there are some mysterious references to isolated Azraqites in the eastern parts of the caliphate at later dates).

The Azraqites stimulated theological thinking because, with a fair measure of logic, they worked out the Khārijite position to an extreme conclusion. The basic principle, which had been formulated in Qur'ānic words by some of ʿAlī's followers who disagreed with him, was: "no decision but God's", that is, "the decision is God's alone"; by this was meant that judgement was to be given in accordance with the Qur'ān.[1] This further implied that all who had committed a grave sin were destined for Hell and belonged to the "people of Hell", since in the Khārijite view this was clearly stated in the Qur'ān. In addition it was held that ʿUthmān had sinned in not inflicting a punishment prescribed in the Qur'ān.

The Azraqites now went still further, on the ground that the existing authorities had also sinned, and asserted that those who did not join their band in fighting the existing authorities were sinners. The members of their band were the true Muslims; their camp alone was the "house of Islam" (*dār al-Islām*) where Islam was truly observed. Those who "sat still" at home and did not make the *hijra* or "migration" to their camp were sinners and unbelievers, outside the community of Islam. This migration, of course, was parallel to the *hijra* of Muḥammad from Mecca to Medina in 622. By thus excluding from the Islamic community even those Muslims who did not agree with them in every detail, they made it lawful to kill such persons, and also their wives and children; for according to old Arab usage there was no wrong in killing someone not a member of one's tribe or an allied tribe, though it would be unwise to do so if the victim's tribe was strong. This puritanical theology became a justification for sheer terrorism, and the Azraqites became noted and feared for their widespread massacres. It is said that when a man went to them and said he wanted to join their band he was given a prisoner to kill; if, as is likely, it was a prisoner from the man's tribe, the killing would break his ties with his tribe and attach him irrevocably to the Azraqites. Doubtless this happened sometimes, but whether it was a regular practice we cannot be certain.

The second sub-sect which became prominent about the same time was the NAJDITES (Najadāt or Najdiyya). The nucleus consisted of Khārijites from central Arabia (from a district called the Yamāma) who helped Ibn-az-Zubayr in Mecca, but later returned to their native region and established a form of autonomous rule. From 686 to 692 their leader was Najda; hence their name. For a time they ruled vast tracts of Arabia—more even than Ibn-az-Zubayr—including Bahrein and Oman ('Umān) on the east coast, and parts of the Yemen and Ḥaḍramawt in the south and south-west. There were many quarrels about the leadership, and after the death of Najda in 692 the sect split up, and the parts either disappeared or were suppressed by the Umayyad generals.

The Najdites originally held views similar to those of the Azraqites, but their responsibility for governing a large territory made them less rigorous in their interpretation. Those who "sat still" and did not actively support them were not regarded as unbelievers (and so outside the community) but only as "hypocrites" (*munāfiqūn*). It is also reported that they authorized members of their sub-sect who lived under non-Khārijite rule to conceal their true opinions—a practice known as *taqiyya* or "prudent fear". Such points show that the Najdites did not have the same clear line of demarcation between themselves and other Muslims as did the Azraqites. Much of the accounts of Najdite views is taken up with legal points of the kind that would naturally arise in the administration of a large state; for example, there were questions about the treatment of captured women by the leaders of an expedition, and about the punishment of isolated cases of theft and adultery.

In what is recorded of Najdite views on such matters

we see the beginnings of a reconsideration of the Khārijite conception of the true Islamic community so as to make allowances for human imperfections. The strict Khārijite view, from which the Najdites presumably started, was that a man who commits a grave sin belongs to the "people of Hell". For the Azraqites living in a camp the man guilty of theft or adultery could easily be excluded from the camp; but it was not easy for the Najdites to banish every thief and adulterer from the entire region which they ruled. They may have thought that it was not even desirable. This was not due to any moral laxity, for they are said to have been strict about wine-drinking, but presumably to the realization that any normal community is bound to contain both good and bad.

It was necessary, however, to find a theoretical justification for the course of action that was practically desirable. This the Najdites did by making a distinction between fundamentals in religion and non-fundamentals. Among the latter they included novel legal points where no official decision had been given. Persistence in theft or adultery was regarded as "idolatry" (*shirk*), presumably on the ground that it implied a false view of the nature of the community and its law or way-of-life. This would be one of the fundamentals, and like errors in the other fundamentals would involve exclusion from the community and inclusion in the "people of Hell". Isolated lapses into theft or adultery, however, were not regarded as affecting fundamentals. The common view that thieves and adulterers went to Hell had therefore to be modified. The Najdites allowed that God might punish them, but insisted that, if he did so, it would not be in Hell, and that he would eventually admit them to Paradise. Thus membership of the community and soundness on fundamentals led to salvation, to Paradise.

While the Azraqites and Najdites were facing the problems of autonomous Khārijite rule, there was a body of moderate Khārijites in Bsara who were concerned rather with the problems of living under non-Khārijite Muslim rule. This body of pious men, with little direct interest in politics, seems to have been in existence throughout the reign of Muʿāwiya. Some of them helped Ibn-az-Zubayr in Mecca for a time; after 684 they accepted, perhaps actively supported, his lieutenant in Basra, and in due course also accepted the Umayyad governor. Unfortunately our information about these people is slight. There appears to have been intense theological activity in Basra about this time, during which the foundations of most later Islamic theology were laid, but we have only tantalizing glimpses of it. It is possible, however, to say something about the chief questions discussed.

The main problem was how to justify the acceptance by Khārijites of a non-Khārijite government. It had been customary for Muslims to distinguish between the "sphere of Islam" (*dār al-islām*) and the "sphere of war" (*dār al-harb*); the former was where the sovereign ruled according to Islamic principles, the latter was where there was no such sovereign and where it was the duty of Muslims to fight if success seemed possible. Neither of these descriptions fitted the position of the moderate Khārijites in Basra. Some therefore spoke of themselves as being in the "sphere of prudent fear", in which they had to conceal their true opinions. This was associated with the view that non-Khārijites were "unbelievers" and "idolaters" (*kāfirūn, mushrikūn*). As time went on, however, it began to seem paradoxical to apply the term "idolaters" to upright God-fearing Muslims who differed from them on a few points. Some therefore allowed that these were at least "monotheists" and that they themselves were living in the "sphere of monotheism". Yet others spoke of their sphere as that of "mixing", and apparently held that, because the government is neither pagan nor strictly Islamic, some things cannot be precisely stated, and a measure of compromise, or rather of indefiniteness and indecision, is necessary.

One of the questions to which much attention was given was that of the marriage of believing women (that is, Khārijites) to "unbelievers" (that is, non-Khārijites), or—what really amounted to the same thing—the sale of believing slave-girls to unbelievers. This raised in a serious form the problem of the relation of the small community of true believers (as they considered it) to the wider community of ordinary "unbelieving" Muslims. According to the Qur'ān a Muslim woman might not marry any but a Muslim man; in other words, her marriage had to be within the community. Since the purchaser of a slave-girl was entitled to have marital relations with her, the sale of a slave-girl to an "unbeliever" made a breach of the Qur'ānic rule likely. The story is told of a man called Ibrāhīm who was kept waiting by a slave-girl and vowed he would sell her to the bedouin. Another member of his sect challenged him, but the majority seems to have gone with Ibrāhīm. That is to say, they decided that they were in some sense members of the wider community. In making this decision they were coming near to abandoning the original Khārijite conception of a "community of saints", which committed no grave sins and held all the right views.

Among the politically quiescent Khārijites of Basra is a small group called the Wāqifites (Wāqifiyya, Wāqifa). Their name means "those who suspend judgement". They were not important in themselves, but they merit attention because they mark a transitional stage between the Khārijites and the Murji'ites (Murji'a), who will be described in the closing chapter of Part

One. It has been noticed above how some even of the morally stricter Khārijites, because they felt that a single lapse into theft or adultery did not deserve to be punished by exclusion from the community, were forced to say that the persons guilty of these crimes would not be punished in Hell. In a sense, then, they were playing down the importance of immoral or anti-social conduct. This was inevitable because of their rigid distinction between the "people of Paradise" and the "people of Hell"; and that distinction was part of the communalistic way of thinking natural to the Arabs. For the pre-Islamic Arab the courage of an individual man had not been simply his own, but also in a sense his tribe's; it was only possible for him to be courageous because he came of courageous stock. The morality of the nomadic Arabs was dominated by loyalty to kin, that is, to one's tribe or clan or family; on behalf of a kinsman almost anything was permitted. This communalistic way of thinking is finding expression in those Khārijites who emphasized the corporate unity of the "people of Paradise" at the expense of certain points of individual morality. In so doing they were going against the more individualistic outlook of the Qur'ān, according to which each man as an individual has to answer for his own sins on the Day of Judgement.

The distinctive position of the Wāqifites was that they suspended judgement on such questions as whether slave-girls should be sold to "unbelievers". In effect they were saying that it is impossible for men to draw a clear dividing-line between the "people of Paradise" and the "people of Hell". This further enabled them to insist that wrongdoers should be punished but not excluded from the community, on the ground that a human being was unable to know their ultimate fate and so had to suspend judgement on it. In this way they countered the tendency to minimize the seriousness of crime and wrongdoing. Thus the Wāqifites and other Khārijites thinking along similar lines were preparing the way for the later Sunnite conception of the Islamic community. They managed to retain something of the old Arab communal outlook and communal feeling, and to attach to the Islamic community as a whole the values formerly attached by the nomad to his tribe. At the same time they made provision for the maintenance of law and order that was essential for the survival of a large civilized community. It is hardly possible to over-estimate the importance of the theological discussions in Basra in the period from about 690 to 730. It was here that the foundations of all later Islamic theology were laid. Why theology should have developed in Iraq, especially Basra, rather than in Syria, Egypt or even Medina, is not clear; but it is a fact, and it is worthy of being further pondered.

There was a Khārijite rising in the north of Iraq in 695–6, and several others during the remainder of the Umayyad period, especially towards its end. These were mostly larger than the risings during the caliphate of Muʿāwiya, and nominally attached to one of the more moderate sub-sects. None of them, however, contributed appreciably to the development of theology. Khārijite doctrines also came to be held by various groups in the Arabian peninsula, North Africa and elsewhere. Some of these, notably the Ibāḍites of Oman, have continued to exist to the present day. The possession of a peculiar doctrine made it easy for small groups to preserve their form of life in almost complete isolation from the world around them. By the end of the Umayyad period, however, and perhaps before then, the Khārijites had ceased to have any contribution to make to the doctrinal development of Islam. What truth there was in their conception of the true Islamic community had been taken over by Murji'ites and others, and their insistence that grave sinners should be excluded from the community had been discredited. By 750 the discussions among the main body of theologically minded Muslims had moved to other topics to which the distinctive Khārijite doctrines were irrelevant.

Bibliography

J. WELLHAUSEN, *Die religiös-politischen Oppositionsparteien im alten Islam*, Göttingen, 1901; thoroughly studies the historical sources for the Khārijites and Shī'ites under the Umayyads. The main risings are also described in his *The Arab Kingdom and its Fall*, Calcutta, 1927.

T. LEWICKI, "Ibāḍīya" in *EI(S)*.

Khārijite sources have recently been studied and interesting results obtained by a group of Italian scholars in Naples. For further references see L. VECCIA VAGLIERI, art. "'Alī b. Abī Ṭālib" in *EI²*; also R. RUBINACCI, art. "Azāriḳa" in *EI²*. Cf. also L. Veccia Vaglieri, "Le Vicende del Harigismo in epoca abbaside", *Rivista degli Studi Orientali*, xxiv (1944), 31-44.

E. A. SALEM, *Political Theory and Institutions of the Khawārij*, Baltimore, 1956; elementary survey.

CHAPTER 3

THE SHI'ITES

ALTHOUGH the Shī'ites and the Khārijites were at opposite poles theologically for most of the Umayyad period, and were in this way complementary, their history was altogether different. Among the Shī'ites there were none of the intellectual debates that took place in Khārijite circles in Basra. For much of the time Shī'ism was quiescent, and anything that was happening was happening under the surface. Then suddenly, when a leader appeared, there would be an explosion. This is perhaps inevitable in a movement which places the emphasis on the leader.

On the death of 'Alī in 661 some of his followers were inclined to support the claims of AL-ḤASAN, the son of 'Alī and Muḥammad's daughter Fāṭima; but al-Ḥasan had no political ability or ambition, and readily gave up his claims in return for the payment of a substantial sum of money by Mu'āwiya. In the troubled period following the death of the latter in 680 al-Ḥasan's full brother AL-ḤUSAYN was encouraged to lead a revolt in Iraq. The promised support was not forthcoming, but al-Ḥusayn and his small band could not be prevailed on to surrender and were eventually massacred by a vastly superior army at Kerbela (Karbalā') in October 680. These tragic events are still annually commemorated by Shī'ites with a kind of Passion Play during the month of Muḥarram—the Arabic month in which the original disaster occurred. In 684 in the confusion of the civil war a group of men from Kufa calling themselves the

Penitents raised an army of 4,000 men, not only to show their penitence but also to avenge al-Ḥusayn. When they marched against an Umayyad force, however, they were utterly defeated. Thus the beginning of the Shīʿite movement was a series of political failures.

The next event in Shīʿite history is slightly more successful and, apart from that, of great significance. This is the rising of AL-MUKHTĀR in Kufa from 685 to 687. Up to this time all the Shīʿites, or at least all the prominent Shīʿites, had been Arabs. In Kufa, however, al-Mukhtār was also joined by *mawāli* or "clients" and, because of tension between the Arabs and the clients, was more and more forced to rely on the latter. Though the rising was crushed by Ibn-az-Zubayr's general, it had sufficient success to give the clients the idea that they had a certain amount of political power if they wielded it aright. A man could become a client in various ways, but the clients intended in this context are probably all non-Arab Muslims. A member of one of the protected communities of Christians, Jews, etc., on becoming a Muslim left his own community and was attached as client to an Arab tribe (presumably because the Islamic community was regarded as a federation of Arab tribes). This was an inferior status, however, in some respects, and as more non-Arabs became Muslims there was a growing volume of dissatisfaction with it and a demand for equality. The clients attracted to Shīʿism appear to have included both persons from the older strata of the population of Iraq (who may be called Aramaeans) and persons of Persian stock. In the Persian empire under the Sasanian dynasty Iraq had been persianized somewhat, while Aramaean culture had spread in Persia proper. In Iraq there was a long tradition of divine kingship, and it would therefore be natural for the Aramaeans in particular to adhere to an Islamic sect which emphasized charismatic leadership.

There were many Persians among the Shī'ites during the Umayyad period, but it must be borne in mind that the close identification of Shī'ism with Persia only dates from the sixteenth century. Nevertheless the rising of al-Mukhtār is an important stage in the development of Islam as a religion, because from this time onwards Shī'ism was linked with the political grievances and aspirations of non-Arab Muslims.

For fifty years after the death of al-Mukhtār in 687 there was no overt political activity among the Shī'ites, though Shī'ite religious ideas were doubtless spreading quietly beneath the surface. There are frequent references to the sub-sect which supported al-Mukhtār, though they are called not Mukhtārites but Kaysānites. This is doubtless a nickname intended to emphasize their non-Arab character, since Kaysān was a prominent client. As signs of collapse became evident in the Umayyad regime, the Shī'ites appear once more on the political stage. Two leaders were executed in Kufa in 737 and another in 742, all suspected of organizing an underground resistance. In 740 there was a serious insurrection under a great-great-grandson of Muḥammad called Zayd, but it was quickly suppressed. Still more serious for the Umayyads was the revolt of 'Abd-Allāh ibn-Mu'āwiya, a great-grandson of Muḥammad's cousin Ja'far; this lasted from 744 to 747. Finally, the movement which replaced the Umayyads by the 'Abbāsids had much Shī'ite support, and on the religious side might be regarded as primarily a manifestation of Shī'ism. It remains to look at the theological developments accompanying these external events.

The first point to be made is that although, as the sources suggest, there may have been widespread sympathy for the Shī'ite position, this position itself was still extremely vague. In particular there was no general recognition that the imāms later acknowledged by the

Imāmite and Ismā'īlite branches of Shī'ism, the descendants of al-Ḥusayn, son of 'Alī, had any special status or special gifts. The tendency was rather to consider that the charismata requisite for the position of imām belonged potentially to all members of Muḥammad's clan of Hāshim, whether descended from Muḥammad through Fāṭima or not. (Descent from Muḥammad never in fact was prominent in Shī'ite claims, but at most secondary, since the position of 'Ali was independent of this.) Thus al-Mukhtār claimed that he was acting on behalf of the imām Muḥammad ibn-al-Hanafiyya ("the son of the Ḥanafite woman"), a son of 'Alı but not by Fāṭima. Some held that the imām after him was his son, Abū-Hāshim. A small group for a time took as imām a great-grandson of al-Ḥasan, known as Muḥammad the Pure Soul (an-Nafs az-Zakiyya). The rising under the great-grandson of Ja'far (Muḥammad's cousin and 'Alī's brother) has already been mentioned. Finally, the 'Abbāsids at first claimed to have inherited the imāmate from Muhammad ibn-al-Ḥanafiyya and Abū-Hāshim, but at a later date (officially from about 780) asserted instead that the true imām after the Prophet was his uncle al-'Abbās, who was of course their ancestor.

Complementary to this acceptance of a variety of men as having the divinely given qualities needed for leadership of the Islamic community there is the fact that no group of importance recognized the descendants of al-Ḥusayn as having any special position. For later Shī'ite theory the first three rightful imāms of the community after Muḥammad are 'Alī, al-Ḥasan and al-Ḥusayn; the fourth is the latter's son 'Alī Zayn-al-'Ābidīn, who died about 712; the fifth is his son Muḥammad al-Bāqir (d. 731); and the sixth his son Ja'far aṣ-Ṣādiq (d. 765). Even Imāmite sources, however, make it clear that these men, the fourth, fifth and sixth imāms, were not active politically; and it would have been difficult for Muslims of this period to conceive of a religious claim that was not also a political one. Nothing at all is recorded of the fourth imām. Of the fifth imām it is reported that the men executed at Kufa in 737 and 742 claimed to be his emissaries; but there is confusion in the stories and it is doubtful if he gave them any support. The sixth imām, Ja'far aṣ-Ṣādiq, seems to have realized the possibilities of a Shī'ite movement and to have set about, doubtless with much caution and circumspection, organizing a body of supporters; but this would mostly take place before the end of the Umayyad period.

The Shī'ism of the Umayyad period was thus vaguer and more indefinite than later Shī'ism, and lacked any semblance of a coherent theory. It was the manifestation of a deep unconscious need—a feeling in men's hearts that they would be happier and more satisfied spiritually if they had a charismatic leader to follow. The imām of whom the Shī'ites dreamed is precisely what is meant by a charismatic leader. The history of early Shī'ism, and indeed of much later Shī'ism also, is that of a pathetic quest for individuals to whom the dignity of imām may be attached. Most of those accepted as imām belied the hopes set on them; and yet the quest went on. The persistence of the quest shows the depth of the feeling involved. Men with political ambitions and qualities of leadership, but no shadow of a claim to the charismata of the Hāshimites, found a way of using this widespread desire for an imām. Al-Mukhtār, for example, asserted that he was acting as the emissary of a genuine imām, Muḥammad ibn-al-Ḥanafiyya; he may have had the consent of the latter in making this assertion, but it is certain that he received no active help from him. There are several later instances of a similar proceeding, and in some of them the imām invoked repudiated the self-styled emissary. Others seem to have resigned themselves to political inactivity in the foreseeable future; and they found a theological justification for this attitude in the theory that the imām was not dead but in concealment and that at an appropriate time he would return as the Mahdī or Guided One (a kind of Messiah) to right all wrongs and establish justice on earth.

Thus Umayyad Shīʿism is a veritable chaos of ideas and attitudes. A beginning of order was introduced by the idea of designation (*naṣṣ*)—this involves the view that there is only one imām at a time and that the imām designates his successor. In the Umayyad period, however, this was not wholly effective, since different groups recognized different imāms. A different line was taken by the Zaydites, the followers of the Zayd who revolted in 740. They would have nothing to do with the idea of a hidden imām; one of the conditions of being imam was that the claim to be such was made publicly (and, of course, was made effective by military success). Zayd's revolt was a realistic attempt to provide an alternative government to that of the Umayyads. He therefore tried to gain the support not merely of the Shīʿites but also of the main body of Muslims, and to do this he made the assertion that, though ʿAlī was the rightful imām after the Prophet and superior to Abū-Bakr and ʿUmar, the "imāmate of the inferior" (*imāmat al-mafḍūl*) was permissible. This concession, however, seems to have alienated the more thorough-going Shīʿites and may have contributed to Zayd's failure.

The ʿAbbāsid movement shows a mixture of genuine religious feeling (though perhaps not in the top leadership) and shrewd political calculation. Realizing how widespread Shīʿite sympathies were, they claimed to be the rightful imāms through inheritance by designation from Muḥammad ibn-al-Ḥanafiyya. Because they saw the weakness of this claim, however, in much of their propaganda they simply called for support for "him of the family of the Prophet who shall be chosen"; and by the time it was made public who this was they were already in power. To gain the Zaydites they maintained that they were seeking vengeance for the blood of Zayd. Another of their aims was the defence of "the weak", which in fact meant the clients or non-Arab Muslims; and actually much of the support for the ʿAbbāsids came from the clients, and their leading general, Abū-Muslim, was himself a client. The volume of support for the ʿAbbāsids from the clients meant that, when they achieved control of the caliphate, clients, especially Persians and persianized Aramaeans, received a due share of power, and the inferior status of the non-Arab Muslims gradually disappears. The success of this at least partly Shīʿite movement in 750 is another stage in the development of Shīʿism, but, as will be seen, its immediate effects are difficult to assess.

Bibliography

J. Wellhausen: works in previous Bibliography.

D. M. Donaldson, *The Shīʿite Religion*, London, 1933; gives the material from the Imāmite sources, but without a full discussion.

I. Friedlaender, "The Heterodoxies of the Shīʿites in the presentation of Ibn Ḥazm", *Journal of the American Oriental Society*, xxviii (1907), 1-80; xxix (1909), 1-183.

S. Moscati, "Per una storia dell' antica Sīʿa", *Rivista degli Studi Orientali*, xxx (1955), 251-67; discusses sources.

CHAPTER 4

THE MURJI'ITES AND OTHER MODERATES

Up to this point the discussion has been of "heretical" sects, and the question naturally arises whether there was at this time a body of "orthodox" opinion and, if so, whether anything more can be said about it. The form of this question, however, is not altogether satisfactory. The term "orthodox" applies in the first place to Eastern Christendom, where there was an authority to say what was "orthodoxy" or "right belief" and what was "heresy". In Islam, however, there was no such authority. There was only the main or central body of opinion in the various schools or sections of the community. In these, too, there was not always the emphasis on the intellectual aspect of religion that there was in Eastern Christendom (though such an emphasis is sometimes found). Thus it is best in Islamic studies to avoid the term "orthodox" and to ask instead whether there was a central body of moderate opinion.

There is not the same objection to the term "heresy". The Arabic term *bid'a* roughly corresponds to the English in effect, though it has a different connotation. *Bid'a* properly means "innovation", and the implication of this term is that the true belief and practice is the original belief and practice—"innovation" is not confined to intellectual matters. This serves to explain why the central body of opinion in Umayyad Islam has not been much studied and why it is difficult to investigate. Muslims of the centre were quite happy to write about the divergent views of the sects; but when it came to the views of their own party they considered that these were in essence identical with those of Muḥammad and his Companions, and therefore they tended to hide any changes and developments or pass them over in silence. There is thus no material for the direct study of this central body, but only large masses of semi-relevant material in biographical dictionaries and similar works —and this still awaits an industrious and keen-sighted investigator.[2]

There is sufficient evidence to make it clear that a central body of moderates in fact existed. Early in the caliphate of ʿAlī there was a body of men in Medina who adopted an attitude of political neutrality; their leader was ʿAbd-Allāh ibn-ʿUmar, the son of the caliph ʿUmar. At a later date modern Western scholars are accustomed to speak of a "pious opposition" in Medina, though its outlines are somewhat hazy. It appears that in the main centres, and notably Medina, Damascus, Basra and Kufa, there were considerable numbers of men who met, probably in the mosques, to discuss religious questions. Most attention seems to have been paid to legal questions (in the Islamic sense which includes liturgical matters); and it is now customary to speak of the "ancient schools" of law. Some groups became specially interested in the spiritual life and asceticism; others occasionally discussed doctrine. During the Umayyad period there was no firm distinction between the different fields of interest, and views in different fields might be reported of the same person. Gradually, however, the fields of law, doctrine and individual piety came to be distinct and separate disciplines, and it became less common for a man to be outstanding in more than one. A fourth discipline also appeared, the science of Tradition, which, especially after 750, became of great importance.

These statements require some expansion. The common view among Muslim scholars has been that the Companions—those Muslims who had seen and talked to Muḥammad—handed on anecdotes about him during their lifetime, and that the anecdotes were then handed on from generation to generation. The anecdotes are technically known as Traditions (always spelt here with a capital), and strict Traditionists always gave a complete *isnād* or list of transmitters, reaching back without a gap to the Companion who heard Muḥammad utter the saying or saw him perform the action. Modern European scholarship, however, rejects this idyllic picture, and considers that for much of the Umayyad period the discussions about law were based on the "living tradition" or consensus of each local school—Medina, Kufa, etc. Only later, perhaps towards the end of the Umayyad period, did one school begin to argue that its teaching on some legal point was superior to that of its rivals because it was based on a Tradition from the Prophet. It was still later, about 800, through the work of the jurist ash-Shāfi'ī (d. 820), that it became the standard practice to justify all legal principles by Traditions. After this, as Muslim scholars themselves recognized, there was much forging of Traditions; often, too, the chain of transmitters, if not exactly forged was at best a conjectural reconstruction. The Muslim scholars devised a critique of Traditions to separate the false from the genuine; but they accepted as "sound" many that European scholars consider forged. They were really interested in the soundness of the practical consequences of the Traditions and not in their historical objectivity in the modern sense.

This means that the standard picture of groups of pious men from the earliest times carefully handing or Traditions with their transmitter-chains is fanciful. Pious men certainly met and talked, and among other things they may have handed on a few stories about Muḥammad, though probably without mentioning the chain of transmitters in full; but they also talked about many other things, and often discussed legal questions purely on the basis of what they conceived to be right and fitting or deducible from Qur'ānic principles. It was only after 800 that it became normal to give a complete chain of transmitters. In the *Life of Muḥammad* by Ibn-Is'ḥāq[3] (who died in 767 or 768), while authorities are frequently mentioned, complete chains are comparatively few. From about 750 we are perhaps justified in speaking of Traditionists and a Traditionist movement, but before 750 it is probably more correct to speak of the "general religious movement". Within this general religious movement with its legal, ascetical and dogmatic aspects there developed a tendency to make use of reason, especially in legal questions. This was found in all the ancient schools, but it came to be particularly associated with Abū-Ḥanīfa (d. 767 or 768) and his followers in Iraq. It was in reaction to this tendency that the Traditionist movement grew up, since many men felt that a Tradition from the Prophet was a sounder basis for action in legal matters than a combination of reasoning and personal opinion or discretion.

There was, then, under the Umayyads this general religious movement with its various aspects. The discussions in Basra about the nature of the community by politically inactive Khārijites and others were part of it. Apart from these questions (to which we shall return presently) one of the chief points of discussion was that of free will and predestination. It has sometimes been suggested that this was due to Christian influence. In a sense this is true, but it did not come about by any external imitation. From about 700 onwards there were among the Muslims men who had been converted from Christianity and who had retained some of their Christian conceptions. As time went on it came to be seen by them and others that these conceptions (which were found in Islam also, but with less emphasis) were relevant to questions which were of concern for the whole Muslim community.

Perhaps the beginning of the discussions about free will was when certain persons argued that, because God determined everything, they could not help committing sins—thus justifying an attitude of moral complacency. A similar line of thought in the political field could lead to the conclusion that the Umayyad regime was ordained by God, sins and all, and was not to be opposed by Muslims. Such arguments would provoke a reaction from those accustomed to think of man as a responsible agent. The root of the belief in free will in Islam is the conviction that God is just; because of his justice he cannot condemn men for actions for which they are not responsible. Some of the Khārijite sects are among the earliest exponents of this line of thought, and it is in accord with their general political attitude of hostility to the Umayyads. The Umayyads and their officials, from this standpoint, are responsible for their sins and misdemeanours, and are unworthy of the sovereignty they exercise; they may also be lawfully opposed when opportunity offers.

The people who held this doctrine of free will were known as QADARITES, because they talked much about *qadar* or had strange ideas about it. *Qadar* means "determination", and is mostly applied to God's effective determination of events—though the ascetic al-Ḥasan al-Baṣrī, to be mentioned presently, asserted that God's "determination" was his "command", that is, to do certain things and to avoid certain others. The term "Qadarite" was actually a nickname, loosely used, which both sides tried to fasten on their opponents. One might have thought that the name was most appropriate for those who maintained God's omnipotence and his *qadar*; but the prevailing usage came to be the application to those who believed in human responsibility and free will. There was no single sect of Qadarites, however, despite the use of the term by some heresiographers, and there was no one who accepted the name for himself.

One of the most important figures in the "general religious movement" was AL-ḤASAN AL-BAṢRĪ (d. 728). He was primarily an ascetic, calling men to self-discipline and uprightness of life in order to avoid divine punishment in the world to come. He was not specially interested in points of doctrine, but doctrinal matters were involved in what he said about preparation for the Last Judgement. His insistence on self-discipline implied man's responsibility for his acts, and he vigorously opposed the complacency fostered by determinism—the attitude expressed by saying "I cannot help sinning for that is how I am made". To this extent he sympathized with the Qadarite position, and he certainly had frequent contacts with Qadarites. It has even been suggested that he was the originator of the Qadarite position, but this seems unlikely. The position had implications of opposition, possibly active opposition, to the Umayyads, and al-Ḥasan did not countenance this. Nor did he share the views of the moderate Khārijites among whom the Qadarite position is found at an early time. On the question of grave sinners he took the view, not that they were excluded from the community, but that they were "hypocrites" (*munāfiqūn*) or as we might say "merely nominal Muslims" and that they were in great danger of Hell and should be encouraged and aided to amend their ways.

Out of the discussions at Basra and elsewhere on the nature of the community and the conditions of membership there eventually arose a new sect, the MURJI'ITES

(Murji'a). The distinctive feature of this sect was that it formally and openly took the step that had almost been taken by those moderate Khārijites who "suspended judgement" on membership of the community; they asserted that the question whether those who had committed grave sins belonged to the "people of Paradise" or the "people of Hell" could not be answered by men but must be left to God's decision on the Last Day. The practical effect of this was that ordinary criminals could be given the prescribed punishments without being expelled from the community. Politically it meant that an Umayyad ruler did not cease to be a member of the community because he did things which some Muslims thought sinful (but which were not clear crimes for which a fixed penalty was prescribed); consequently revolt against the Umayyads was not lawful. Thus the Murji'ites were first and foremost a party which supported the Umayyads on religious grounds; though they may not have had much enthusiasm for the Umayyads, they recognized the importance of law and order.

Despite this general attitude of support for the Umayyad government it may be that towards the end of the period some Murji'ites felt that it had become intolerable and ought to be opposed. At least a man called GHAYLĀN from Damascus, usually called a Murji'ite, was executed by the caliph Hishām (*regnabat* 724–43). The reason for the execution is given as the holding of Qadarite views; and this probably means that Ghaylān had been engaging in subversive political activity. To hold that insurrection is right in certain circumstances is, of course, not incompatible with the general Murji'ite view that grave sins do not exclude from the community.

Even in the scanty reports that have come to us about the Murji'ites there is much more than this. They did not simply contradict Khārijite views. They developed positively a conception of "faith" (*īmān*) as that which constitutes a man a member of the community, and in accordance with this they speak of the "sphere" in which they live as the "sphere of faith". In their teaching no distinction was made between "faith" and *islām* or external adhesion to the community, though sections of the Traditionist movement (probably later) held that "faith" meant something more than being externally a Muslim.[4] The Murji'ite conception of faith was held with various degrees of elaboration. One of the fullest definitions is that of Abū-Ḥanīfa that faith consists in knowledge of God and public acknowledgement of him together with knowledge of the Messenger (Muḥammad) and acknowledgement of what was revealed through him. It is difficult to compare this with Christian conceptions of faith. These refer to man's relation to God, but the point at issue for Muslim theologians is what makes a man one of the community of "believers" (or "faithful")—the word used is the participle, *mu'minūn*, corresponding to the Arabic word for "faith", *īmān*. Emphasis is placed on the intellectual content, and works are omitted, since the aim is to avoid having to exclude a man from the community because he has sinned. This is not unlike the "orthodoxy" of the Byzantines, but it is not identical. What a man has to know and acknowledge is not only the being of God but also what was revealed to Muḥammad; and this includes the whole Islamic way of life.

The great achievement of Islamic theology during the Umayyad period is thus the clarification of the conception of the community. The Khārijite idea of a community of saints proved itself unworkable in practice. Not without difficulty it was replaced by the Murji'ite conception, according to which the community was based on certain beliefs about the nature of God and on the acceptance of a divinely instituted way of life. This is in essentials the conception of the main body of the Sunnites, and indeed of most Muslims ever since. The one difference is that they usually placed less emphasis on the beliefs about God, and regarded the acceptance and public profession of them as a part of the Sharīʿa or revealed way of life.

Bibliography

I. GOLDZIHER, *Die Ẓāhiriten*, Leipzig, 1884, esp. 3-20; discusses the relation of rational methods in law to the Traditionist movement. There is a full discussion of the Traditionist movement in Goldziher's *Mohammedanische Studien*, ii (Halle, 1890).

Joseph SCHACHT, *The Origins of Muhammadan Jurisprudence*, Oxford, 1950; a very important work, chiefly concerned with ash-Shāfiʿī, but reviewing the earlier period. The author's conclusions are expressed more briefly in *Esquisse d'une histoire du droit musulman*, Paris, 1953, and in *Law in the Middle East*, edited by M. Khadduri and H. J. Liebesny (Washington, 1955), i. 28-84.

H. H. SCHAEDER, "Ḥasan al-Baṣrī . . .", *Der Islam*, xiv (1925), 1-75; H. RITTER, "Studien zur Geschichte der islamischen Frömmigkeit: I. Ḥasan al-Baṣrī", *Der Islam*, xxi (1933), 1-83. The former deals with political relationships, the latter with the teaching.

J. OBERMANN, "Political Theology in Early Islam: Ḥasan al-Baṣrī's Treatise on Qadar", *Journal of the American Oriental Society*, lv (1935), 138-62; expounds the document published by Ritter.

Part Two

THE FIRST WAVE OF HELLENISM 750–950

THE HISTORICAL BACKGROUND

ONE of the main factors which enabled the ʿAbbāsid dynasty to win the caliphal power was the support of Persian clients. It was therefore not surprising that after the establishment of the ʿAbbāsids many of the subordinate offices in the administration and much of the actual power was in the hands of Persians or persianized Aramaeans. The outstanding example is the power of the Persian family of Barmak (the Barmakids or Barmecides), whose head was vizier from 786 to 803. The transference of the capital of the caliphate from Damascus to Iraq—to Baghdad after its foundation in 763—affected the internal distribution of power. In effect it meant that the main work of administration was in the hands of the class of "secretaries" or civil servants, who had continued to exist as a class since before the Muslim conquest and retained much of the technique of government of the Persian empire under the Sasanians. These men, too, were the bearers of the Persian or rather persianized culture of Iraq. Some were Christians, others Zoroastrians; but Zoroastrianism, because it was the official religion and almost a department of government, was in decline as a religion. Thus the secretaries had a culture of which they were proud, including important Hellenistic elements, but, apart from the Christians, they had little vital religion. When they saw the best appointments in their profession going to Muslims, many of them accepted Islam.

The ʿAbbāsids, however, had also had the support of sections of the "general religious movement", especially those interested in legal questions. Apparently they respected their views, and were prepared to select judges from the ranks of these men. At the same time they brought pressure to bear on them to overcome their disagreements and form a common outlook. Part of the evidence for this is some advice given to the caliph al-Manṣūr (754–75) in a letter by a Persian secretary, Ibn-al-Muqaffaʿ (d. 759), who is incidentally one of the creators of Arabic prose.[1] This man also exemplifies a conflict which was intimately linked with the development of Islamic theology—the conflict between the old secretary class and the new class of religious intellectual which was forming within the "general religious movement" and which may by anticipation be called the class of ulema (*ʿulamāʾ*) or scholar-jurists. While the main struggle may be said to have been for positions of power within the ʿAbbāsid administration, this had many ramifications, especially in the intellectual field. Thus Ibn-al-Muqaffaʿ is the author of an attack on the Qurʾān, which was of course the basis of the thinking of the rival class.[2] His best-known work is his translation into Arabic of *Kalīla and Dimna*, which is a treasury of Indian and other eastern wisdom, appearing in different forms and with different names in several languages; perhaps his aim was to offer this as an alternative to the Qurʾān.

Ibn-al-Muqaffaʿ adopted a standpoint which may be labelled Manichaean; and for a time some secretaries probably found Manichaeanism a useful basis from which to oppose the emergent class of ulema, and indeed their Muslim masters generally. From about 779 to 786, however, there was an official persecution of *zindīqs* or "dualistic heretics", which was largely directed against Manichaeanism of this type; and after that period we hear less of Manichaeanism among the secretaries. Other ways were then found of stating their case. One was the Shuʿūbite movement, which aimed at the depreciation of all things Arab; but this was mainly a literary and not a theological movement, and need not be further considered here. What was more important was that the secretaries turned to philosophy, in which some of them had perhaps always been versed. Philosophy belonged to the system of Hellenistic education which had been established in Iraq under the Sasanians and was continued under the Muslims. The main subject of this system of education was probably medicine; but philosophy and other "Greek sciences" were always taught as well. This education was mainly in the hands of Christians, the best-known college being one at Gundē-Shāpur (about a hundred miles north-east of Basra). Later, when a hospital was set up in Baghdad, there were probably philosophical lectures in connection with the medical teaching. This system of Hellenistic education was thus complete in itself, and spread over a number of institutions. When a new system of Islamic education arose out of the "general religious movement", it was completely separate, and until after 1100 did not contain any of the disciplines of the Hellenistic system.

Apart from this matter of the civil service, the establishment of ʿAbbāsid rule, following on the disorder of the last twenty years of the Umayyad period, brought economic expansion and widespread prosperity. Gradually, however, it became more and more difficult for the caliph and the central administration to keep a firm grip on the provinces. Almost immediately Spain slipped from their grasp into that of a branch of the Umayyad family. Elsewhere after a time they found themselves compelled to appoint their provincial governors for life, and then to appoint their sons after them. One of the earliest examples of this was the Ṭāhirid family which ruled Khurasan with virtual autonomy from 820 to 872, though in name they were vassals of the caliph. They were displaced, by force of arms, by another dynasty, the Ṣaffārids, whose rule had originally been based still farther to the east. They in turn had to yield to the Sāmānids, who had been governors of Transoxiana before bringing much of Persia also under their sway. Their effective rule is reckoned as lasting from 874 to 999. Similar things were happening in North Africa and elsewhere.

Yet more serious was the loss of power in the central region itself. This proceeded *pari passu* with the gaining of autonomy by the provinces. At last in 936 the caliph of the day had to acknowledge a comparatively unimportant war-lord Ibn-Rā'iq as "prince of princes" (or perhaps "commander-in-chief") and virtual ruler of Baghdad. In 945 this man was replaced by the Persian family of the Buwayhids or Būyids, who were able to retain control of most of the central regions of the caliphate until 1055, though latterly with a weakening grasp.

CHAPTER 5

THE TRANSLATORS AND THE FIRST PHILOSOPHERS

SHORTLY after the inauguration of the 'Abbāsid caliphate, translations into Arabic began to be made of Greek scientific and philosophical works. At first the choice of works depended probably on the individual scholar or his patron, but the caliph AL-MA'MŪN (813–833) or his advisers realized the importance for the whole empire of the Greek sciences and organized the work of translation on a large scale. An institution was set up called the "House of Wisdom" (*bayt al-ḥikma*), where books were translated and copied, and where a library was kept for reference. For a period of a century or two translations continued to be made, and the older translations revised. The greatest name is that of ḤUNAYN IBN-IS'ḤĀQ (809–73), a Christian from al-Ḥīra who became a teacher of medicine in Baghdad and court physician to the caliph al-Mutawakkil (*regnabat* 847–61). He had something like a bureau for translation, with several well-qualified colleagues. Unlike most of the earlier translators—nearly all Iraqian Christians—who had translated from Syriac, Ḥunayn had learnt Greek and was in the habit of collating a number of manuscripts before making his translations. This was the highest level reached by the translators from the technical and linguistic standpoint. Later, however, with the growth of independent philosophical thinking in Arabic, the translations were revised to express the arguments with greater clarity, precision and accuracy; but this was usually done from Syriac versions and not from the Greek originals.

The vast extent of the work of translation is impressive. Both the translations still extant and the greater number whose titles only are known are listed according to the Greek authors in *Die arabischen Ubersetzungen aus dem Griechischen*, by Moritz Steinschneider (p. xvii above). At first sight it looks as if all Greek works on science and philosophy had been translated into Arabic; but this is not so. Recent studies have shown that what in fact was translated was that section of Greek scientific and philosophical literature which was still valued in the late Hellenistic schools. This includes the whole of Aristotle except the *Politics*; even the *Poetics* was translated, though one wonders how intelligible it was to men who had no acquaintance with drama. The pre-Socratics were neglected, but some later writers received more attention than has been the case in the modern European tradition; indeed philosophical works of Galen have been preserved in Arabic which are not extant in Greek. Thus the translations of Greek works throw light not merely on the origins of philosophy in Arabic, but also on the later history of Greek science and philosophy in Hellenistic times.

All this work of translation, especially in philosophy, is only possible where there is contact with a living tradition. The great theologian al-Ghazālī claims that he mastered the philosophy of his day solely from books. This is doubtless true with regard to the advanced stages, and is an indication of the complete isolation of Islamic education from that in the so-called "foreign sciences"; but al-Ghazālī was already well versed in somewhat similar theological disciplines and may have had some elementary teaching in philosophy, so that he was not wholly out of touch with a living tradition. In the early ʿAbbāsid period there seem to have been two main lines of tradition influencing the Islamic world. Firstly, there was that of Gundē-Shāpur. From 765 to 870 the Persian-Nestorian family of Bokhtīshū' from this centre supplied the court physician to the caliphs, and at the same time were responsible for a teaching hospital in Baghdad. Besides the strictly medical curriculum there must also have been some work in philosophy here. Secondly there was the philosophical tradition of Alexandria. The fact that before the Arab conquest Syriac had been replacing Greek suggests that it was not in a healthy condition—perhaps because of the rising "nationalism" of the Copts or their unmetaphysical outlook. Whatever the reason—and it may be connected with the weakness of Islamic intellectual life in Egypt—about 718 the college was moved to Antioch. Here it remained for over a century, but about 850 migrated eastwards to Ḥarrān, along the road to Mosul, and then about half a century later was attracted to the metropolis, Baghdad. These migrations were primarily migrations of the teachers and also to some extent of the library. In Baghdad they seem to have taken a full share in the intellectual life of the capital or at least that section of it which was sympathetic to philosophy.

There were also other lines of philosophical tradition, but we are not so well informed about them. Besides the Alexandrian college in Ḥarrān, which was under Christian direction, there was a pagan centre belonging to the sect known as the Ṣābi'ans. Their religion included star-worship, but it had a basis in Greek philosophy, and in consequence of this they made important contributions to the arabizing of the Hellenistic intellectual tradition. In 872 one of their leading scholars, THĀBIT IBN-QURRA (d. 901), who had already studied at Baghdad, quarrelled with other members of the sect and left Ḥarrān for the capital. Here with support from the caliph he devoted himself to translating and to composing original works, chiefly in medicine and mathematics; he also collected round him some younger Ṣābi'ans. It was not only in Baghdad, however, that philosophy was cultivated. The biographies of some of the leading philosophers makes it clear that there was also considerable interest in it in the eastern part of the caliphate; but it is not possible to say anything definite about this.

After thus noticing the extent of the work of translating and the interest in philosophy, it is worth pausing to ask what attracted the Muslims so strongly to it. There was obviously a practical interest. The caliphs were concerned for their own health and that of those around them, and believed that the practitioners of Greek medical science could do something to help them. It must also be remembered that in the *milieu* with which we are concerned a high practical value was attached to astrology, which was not distinguished from astronomy. Astrological-astronomical works had an important place in the translation programme, and those competent in this discipline were received with favour at court. Since philosophy was closely associated with these sciences, it was natural that attention should be paid to it also. It is probable, however, that long before the time of al-Ma'mūn and the organization of translations, the more thoughtful of the Muslims in the "general religious movement" had begun to realize the importance of logical methods, and of philosophy as a whole, in arguments with members of other religions. There must have been much argument of this kind. Among the works of Saint John of Damascus (d. 750) is a "Disputation between a Christian and a Saracen" which was probably intended to show Christians the arguments they were likely to meet and possible lines of reply to them. A record has also been preserved of the speech made by the Nestorian patriarch Timothy in 781 in a public discussion in the presence of the caliph. This makes it clear that from a very early date the Muslims must have realized that they were living among people of higher intellectual culture who rejected and criticized some of their religious beliefs. Apart from Christians and other religious bodies found in Iraq they were probably in contact with Buddhists and members of Indian sects. Thus the needs of polemics and apologetics supplied a strong reason for the study of philosophy, and in addition there is the tension between the class of secretaries and the new class of ulema.

How exactly the transition was made from translation to the composition of original works is not altogether clear. It would be natural, however, for some of the scholars engaged in translation to want to write something original, either to add something to what was in the Greek works, or to provide a simple introduction for those unfamiliar with the Greek sciences. There was also a need to bring philosophical conclusions more into line with Islamic doctrines. This transition and these motives are exemplified in Abū-Yūsuf Ya'qūb ibn-Is'ḥāq AL-KINDĪ (*c.* 800–70). He is usually known as al-Kindī, and, as the first of the notable Islamic philosophers and the only one of Arabic descent, he is also called the "philosopher of the Arabs" (*faylasūf al-'Arab*). The last reason for original philosophical writing was perhaps the most important, and his production has been described as essentially "Greek philosophy for Muslims".[3]

Al-Kindī's family had held a number of official posts in Arab parts of the caliphate; the chief of these had been the governorship of Kufa. He himself became attached to the caliphal court, and during the reign of al-Mu'taṣim (833–42) was tutor to the latter's son. This was during the period of the Mu'tazilites' ascendancy (to be described in the next chapter), and al-Kindī seems to have shared their views on dogmatic questions. In this respect he was much closer to the main body of Islamic theological thought than most of the other philosophers. Early in the reign of al-Mutawakkil (847–61) there was a reversal of government policy and the Muʿtazilites fell from favour. This may have contributed to an unfortunate experience which befell al-Kindī; by the intrigues of two hostile courtiers his library was taken from him and removed to Basra for a time, but in the end he got it back again.

From this incident we know that al-Kindī had what was for the time a huge library. He must have spent the greater part of his time in study, and was an acknowledged expert in nearly all the Greek sciences. His numerous short writings suggest that he was an effective agent in spreading the knowledge of these sciences among the Muslims. The philosophical position which he adopted was by and large Neoplatonic, as was that of most of the Islamic philosophers. This was mainly the result of the form taken by the later Greek philosophical tradition when the Muslims came into contact with it. Though Aristotle was studied carefully, he was seen through Neoplatonic eyes. To increase the confusion there was a work in circulation among the Muslims known as *The Theology of Aristotle*, which has now been recognized as consisting of extracts from the Neoplatonic philosopher Plotinus. This work had a considerable vogue in its Arabic version. Its Neoplatonic doctrine of God must have seemed sufficiently close to Qur'ānic monotheism. At any rate al-Kindī accepted Neoplatonism with what must have seemed to him minor modifications. He felt capable of asserting that the truths revealed through prophets were metaphysical knowledge, and that there was no contradiction between philosophy and revelation.[4] Presumably he meant that philosophy could be developed in a way that was both in accordance with its own nature and also compatible with revelation. He did not simply take over the views of others, but into the Neoplatonic doctrine of emanation quietly inserted a creation out of nothing, as if there was no difficulty in reconciling the two.

If, then, al-Kindī's work may be characterized as an attempt to produce a version of Greek philosophy for Muslims, the reason for this is to be found in his association with the Muʿtazilites and in the political situation of his early maturity. From about 833 to 849, as will be seen later, the theologians of the Muʿtazilite sect were closely associated with the work of government; they were men belonging to the "general religious movement" but were perhaps trying to bring about a reconciliation with the secretary class. About 849 there was a change in government policy, and support was sought rather from what was now fully developed as the Traditionist wing of the "general religious movement". The Traditionists were in the main hostile to philosophy; and it is not surprising that for the next two hundred years philosophy is cultivated almost exclusively by the secretary class and other rivals of the Traditionists and theologians. The two great names in the Neoplatonic line of thought pioneered by al-Kindī are al-Fārābī (d. 950) and Avicenna (d. 1037); the former of these will be more conveniently treated in the next chapter.

Meanwhile there is another important name to be noticed in the early ʿAbbāsid period, that of AR-RĀZĪ (that is, the man from Rayy), well known in Europe as Rhazes. His full name is Abū-Bakr Muḥammad ibn-Zakariyyā' ar-Rāzī, and he is said to have been born in 865 and to have died in 923 or 932. His early life was spent in his native town of Rayy (near the modern Teheran), and it was only after his thirtieth birthday that he began to study medicine in Baghdad. He practised as a physician and taught both at Rayy and

Baghdad and also for short periods at some of the minor courts in the eastern regions of the caliphate.

His chief claim to fame is as a physician, and his medical works were long read and valued in Europe. Yet like most physicians of this period he was also something of a philosopher. Indeed philosophy might be said to take the place of religion for him, as it did for Plato, whom he greatly admired and tended to follow. It was through philosophy and the use of reason, he believed, that human life could be improved. This outlook finds expression in a simply written little book on ethics and the art of living, which has been translated into English under the title of *The Spiritual Physick*. The translator speaks of his attitude as one of "intellectual hedonism", which "reflects very characteristically the outlook of the cultured Persian gentleman". He had little use for religion, Islamic or any other. Doubtless he shared something of the outlook of the Persian secretary class, of whom he must have known many; but, though he is said to have had Manichaean sympathies, there is no clear evidence of this in his writings. Likewise, he is said to have had connections with the Ṣābi'an philosophical school of Ḥarrān; but his philosophy is more Platonic than either Neopythagorean (like that of the Ṣābi'ans) or Neoplatonic. Its precise source is, indeed, still something of a mystery, and he stands apart from the other Islamic philosophers. His ideal of life was of one devoted to intellectual pursuits, and his philosophy was of a piece with this. The ideal could not be made universal, but the philosophy justified his own use of his talents in helping to raise the level of Islamic culture, even if it was not a satisfactory account of what he in fact achieved.

Bibliography

For the translators cf. *GAL*, i. 219-29; *GALS*, i. 362-71; Graf, *GCAL*, ii. 109-14, 122-32, etc.

STEINSCHNEIDER (p. xvii above) arranges the translations according to the authors translated.

Max MEYERHOF, "Von Alexandrien nach Bagdad: ein Beitrag zur Geschichte des philosophischen und medizinischen Unterrichts bei den Arabern", *Sitzungsberichte der preussischen Akademie der Wissenschaften*, Berlin, 1930, Phil. hist. Kl., 389-429.

J. SCHACHT and M. MEYERHOF, *The Medico-Philosophical Controversy between Ibn Buṭlan of Baghdad and Ibn Riḍwan of Cairo*, Cairo, 1937.

B. SPULER, "Hellenistisches Denken im Islam", *Speculum*, v. (1954). 179-93.

R. WALZER, *Greek into Arabic*, Oxford, 1962; important articles reprinted.

AR-RĀZĪ, *The Spiritual Physick*, tr. by A. J. Arberry, London (Wisdom of the East Series), 1950.

CHAPTER 6

THE EXPANSION OF SHĪʿISM

THE Shīʿism of the first two ʿAbbāsid centuries has not been adequately studied. This is partly due to the great difficulty of the subject. Many of the real events took place "underground", and several different stories were made public, none of which is necessarily true. There are Sunnite versions and Shīʿite versions. The Sunnite versions tend to put everything in a bad light; but the Shīʿite accounts are perhaps even less helpful to the modern historian. There is a strong tendency among the Shīʿites, though it is not unknown elsewhere in Islam, to appear to be discussing past history when in fact one is discussing contemporary politics. There are apparently endless discussions about what happened in 632 on the death of Muḥammad or in 656 when ʿAlī became caliph, but what the disputants are interested in are the political principles to be followed in the middle of the ninth century. For reasons that can only be surmised this was the form taken by political discussions under the ʿAbbāsids. To complicate matters, many of these allegations about the past were taken at their face value by the heresiographers and fitted into a historical scheme centred in the persons of the imāms or leaders. This gives the impression of a single great Shīʿite movement, splitting into separate factions at various points, whereas the truth is rather that there were numerous local movements unconnected with one another until the heresiographers linked them. It is thus understandable that little progress has been made in disentangling the great mass of detail.

The most important instance of some of the features mentioned is in respect of the recognition of the twelve imāms of the Imāmite branch of Shī'ism. The impression given by Shī'ite writers, and even by Sunnite heresiographers, is that during their lives they were recognized by a wide circle of followers, indeed by most of the Shī'ite movement. Scrutiny of the Shī'ite accounts of the imāms, however, makes it clear that most of them were politically insignificant, and were not really recognized by anyone at all. JA'FAR AṢ-ṢĀDIQ (d. 765) may have been dabbling in politics before the fall of the Umayyads, and hoping to gain a position of rule; he doubtless realized that political capital was to be made out of the charisma of being a member of the "family" (*ahl al-bayt*). After the 'Abbāsids had established themselves, however, he saw the obvious dangers for himself of political activity, and refrained. His son Mūsā took the same line. Another son Ismā'īl, however, went ahead and began the process of fusing together several underground revolutionary movements, with results that will be seen presently.

Mūsā (d. 799) and his branch of the "family" remained politically quiescent until in 817 the caliph al-Ma'mūn married his daughter to Mūsā's son 'Alī ar-Riḍā and declared him heir to the caliphate. This was part of a policy designed to gain further support for the government from persons of Shī'ite sympathies. Unfortunately 'Alī died in 818. His young son Muḥammad continued in favour at the court of al-Ma'mūn, but died in 835 soon after the latter's death. His son 'Alī an-Naqī was imprisoned as a consequence of the great change of policy about 849, and remained in prison until his death in 868. In turn his son al-Ḥasan al-'Askarī was imprisoned for a time after his father's death, but then set free. Soon after his death in 874 the twelfth imām, his son Muḥammad, either died or disappeared, but the majority of the

Shīʿites came to believe that he would one day return as al-Mahdī, the Guided One, a figure roughly corresponding to the Jewish Messiah.

From this brief recital, based on Imāmite sources, it is seen that during the lifetime of these men there was no organized movement accepting a member of this branch of the "family" as imām. An otherwise suspicious government was not unduly worried, and may have used the imprisonment, which was far from harsh, as a method of exercising surveillance. It follows from this that during the ninth century up to 874 the main body of Shīʿism—assuming there was such a main body—was not a body of people recognizing the imāms who have been named. The little groups of people professing to follow these imāms, living or dead, or other members of the "family", may be neglected. Apart from these there was a number of respectable theologians, calling themselves Shīʿites (but usually called Rāfiḍites or "deserters" by their opponents), who shared fully in the intellectual life of Baghdad and do not seem to have been politically suspect. The best known was Hishām ibn-al-Ḥakam, who was active from the end of the eighth century until 825 or later. What can the Shīʿism of such a person have amounted to?

The chief doctrine held by these Rāfiḍites, and their successors the Imāmites (or Ithnāʿasharites or "Twelvers"), was that ʿAlī had been clearly designated imām or leader of the community by Muḥammad in succession to himself. This implied that such designation by the preceding imām was the proper title to succession. Since the imām was further held to be divinely preserved from error, Shīʿite doctrine was encouraging a very autocratic form of government. (The word "imām" thus in effect means "caliph" or "rightful caliph", but with the Shīʿites, who favoured it, it had the further connotation of divinely given charismata.)

A corollary of the main doctrine was that most of Muḥammad's Companions (who have a special place of honour in Islam) had disobeyed his order in not recognizing 'Alī as caliph on his death; and a consequence of this was that they were not fit persons to transmit Traditions about him. In this way the Rāfiḍites were undermining the elaborate structure of Tradition, the basis of the Sharī'a or Islamic law, and thereby the power and influence of the growing class of ulema—Traditionists and jurists.

Thus this moderate Shī'ism of the early ninth century can be regarded as the intellectual expression of a widespread mentality or outlook, not sufficiently organized to be called a party. One might perhaps speak of the "autocratic bloc", provided it is understood that the persons included in this are not exactly known. On the religious side it would include those who looked to a charismatic leader for salvation and security, and whose politics were affected by this desire. It would also include groups moved by more strictly political interests, the class of secretaries and all the old Persian nobility now involved in the work of administration, and possibly others also. Opposed to this bloc one will postulate a "constitutional bloc", which will include the ulema and all those whose share in power and influence is linked with the development of the Islamic sciences; they are "constitutionalists" in so far as the autocratic power of the caliph and those who are able to act in his name is diminished by the existence of the Sharī'a. On the religious side the need felt is for a charismatic community rather than for a charismatic leader.

At numerous points in the earlier history of Shī'ism the messianic ideas endemic in the Middle East had attached themselves to one or other of the many persons recognized as imām by some small group. After 874 it occurred to certain political leaders of the autocratic bloc that it would be advantageous to have, instead of a living imām, one whose whereabouts were unknown and whose return, though it would happen eventually, was not expected in the visible future. This satisfied men's religious aspirations and also gave the politicians a free hand. On the basis of the recognition of the Twelve Imāms many of the distinct groups with Rāfiḍite sympathies were fused into something like a party; and from this time the party or sect is usually called the Imāmites. In this work of organization a prominent part was played by Abū-Sahl Ismāʿīl an-Nawbakhtī (d. 923).[5] We also hear of the specifically Imāmite form of Islamic law being founded about this time. The end of the ninth century is thus the period in which Imāmite Shīʿism took definite shape.

In the immediately following period it had some successes. Al-Ashʿarī, probably writing about 920, says that it is dominant in the Idrīsid state of Morocco and in the towns of Qumm and Kufa.[6] Soon afterwards it became dominant in the Ḥamdānid state in Syria, while in 945 the Shīʿite Buwayhid war-lords became virtual rulers in Baghdad. What exactly lies behind these events is difficult to say, but it would perhaps not be far wrong to say that Shīʿism was closely linked with the desire for a more autocratic form of government. Some insight into the intellectual outlook that went with Shīʿism is provided by the thought of one of the great Arabic-writing philosophers, who spent the last few years of his life under the protection of Sayf-ad-Dawla of Aleppo.

This was AL-FĀRĀBĪ (875–950), known as "the second Teacher" (Aristotle being the first). Though born in Turkistan he eventually studied philosophy and the Greek sciences in Baghdad. How he gained a livelihood is not clear. Since he lived an ascetic life, his requirements were doubtless few. His philosophy may be described as having a foundation of Aristotelianism, and a superstructure of Neoplatonic metaphysics. To this he added a political theory based on the study of Plato's *Republic* and *Laws*. The last element seems to be an original contribution of his own, but in the former two he is developing the line of thought of al-Kindī. In the centre of his metaphysics is the First Being or absolute One, which was understood to be identical with God as proclaimed in Islamic doctrine. From him emanated all other existent things in hierarchical order. Similarly in the state there is a head, the *ra'īs*, from whom all authority in the state emanates in that he assigns men to their appropriate grades (in something the same way as the ʿAbbāsid caliph assigned men to various posts in the court and the administration). The grades are described as grades of commanding and obeying or of controlling and being controlled. At the top is the *ra'īs* who controls others but is not himself controlled; at the foot in the lowest grade are those who are themselves controlled but do not control any others below them. The intermediate grades control others and are themselves controlled in varying degrees.

Al-Fārābī uses perfectly general terms (like "head" rather than imām or caliph) which could be applied to non-Islamic states as well as to the Islamic empire, but he is thinking primarily of the Islamic world. The "first head" of his ideal state is a prophet who has also the best qualities of the true philosopher. He is to be followed by a "second head" who should have slightly different qualities. What is said about the "second head" could be interpreted in such a way as to make him more or less identical with an Imāmite imām; and that would mean that al-Fārābī's philosophy could be regarded as providing a basis for Imāmite Shīʿism. This would make him acceptable in Shīʿite Aleppo. Whether this is his own dominant view, however, is not clear; for he goes on to say that, if the qualities necessary for the "second head" are not all found in one man, then rule may be divided among those who share the qualities; and among those who thus share authority are some whose descriptions correspond to the Traditionists and ulema (as they were in Baghdad in the early tenth century). Perhaps al-Fārābī really tried to keep aloof from the conflict between Shīʿism and Sunnism and the underlying struggle of rival interests, and was chiefly concerned that philosophy should be fully used to improve conditions in the caliphate.

The Imāmite branch of Shīʿism was not the only one that took definite shape about this period. After the break between Jaʿfar aṣ-Ṣādiq and his son Ismāʿīl (perhaps about 760), the latter, with his son Muḥammad and other helpers, set about creating a revolutionary Shīʿite movement out of a number of groups of discontented persons in various parts of the caliphate. The movement was of course "underground", and this leads to many obscurities in its history. The Ismāʿīlites had a series of "hidden imāms", but in contrast to the Imāmites they were, at least at times, in effective contact with their imām, and under his supervision in the work of propaganda. This appears to have extended to Iraq, Syria, the Yemen and North Africa. Success eventually came in North Africa, and what is known as the Fāṭimid state was set up in 909 in Tunisia under a man who claimed to be a descendant of Ismāʿīl. In 969 it conquered Egypt, and the new capital of Cairo was built. Meanwhile a closely connected movement, the Qarmaṭians (Qarāmiṭa, Carmathians), established a semi-independent principality at Bahrein on the east coast of Arabia. Little is known about Ismāʿīlite doctrine, however, until some time after 950; so this may be left to a later chapter.

Bibliography

Bernard Lewis, *The Origins of Ismāʿilism*, Cambridge, 1940; clarifies many obscure problems, and is generally accepted.

W. Ivanow, *The Rise of the Fatimids*, London, 1942; differs from Lewis; gives texts and translations.

W. Montgomery Watt, "The Rāfiḍites: a preliminary Study", in *Oriens* (1962).

CHAPTER 7

THE MU'TAZILITES

In the latter part of the nineteenth century European scholars were attracted by some of the views of the Mu'tazilites and studied them with great sympathy. In an account of them published in 1865 Heinrich Steiner of Zürich spoke of them as "the free-thinkers of Islam". At this period there was no appreciation in Europe of the philosophical theology that later became dominant. The Mu'tazilites stood for freedom of the will and human responsibility; in other respects they adopted sensible, almost nineteenth-century-liberal attitudes. It was felt that Islam would have been ever so much more congenial to the European if only the Mu'tazilites had not been replaced by the dry-as-dust, hide-bound, hair-splitting Ash'arites and their like. As further knowledge was gained, however, it was realized that this whole conception of the Mu'tazilites was inaccurate. They were not free-thinkers but quite definit Muslims, even if they indulged in speculation on some points; and, far from being liberal in outlook, they were at the back of the unhappy episode of the "Inquisition" in the early ninth century. In time it was further realized that they were zealous apologists for Islam towards members of other religions. They were also involved in the politics of their day, but what preciselyheir attitudes were is not yet agreed.

First and foremost the Mu'tazilites who are important in the history of Islamic theology are the persons responsible for initiating the discussion of Islamic dogmas in terms of Greek philosophical conceptions. They differ from the philosophers—although al-Kindī was close to them in outlook—in that they accept Islamic dogma in detail. Originally the name was applied fairly widely, and seems to have included all who discussed dogmatic questions philosophically; but by about 900 it was restricted to those who, in addition to employing "philosophical" methods, accepted the five points of the Muʿtazilite dogmatic position (to be enumerated later). Thus a man called Ḍirār ibn-ʿAmr (who was probably active from 790 or earlier until about 810) is sometimes called a Muʿtazilite. He is said to have been the chief exponent of philosophical theology in Basra before Abu-'l-Hudhayl, and apparently knew enough about the Greeks to write a critique of the Aristotelian doctrine of substances and accidents.[7] He did not accept the usual Muʿtazilite doctrine of human free will, however, and was disavowed by the Muʿtazilites, at least before the end of the ninth century. Perhaps because of this disavowal and because no later theologians held his views (though he was in some respects a predecessor of the Ashʿarites), little has been recorded about his life and doctrines.

The main founders of the Muʿtazilite theological position were four men: Muʿammar (or Maʿmar), Abū-'l-Hudhayl and an-Naẓẓām at Basra and Bishr ibn-al-Muʿtamir at Baghdad. The dates of their deaths are given as 830, 841 (or later), 846 and 825; but not too much reliance can be placed upon these as a guide to the period of their chief activity. Abū-'l-Hudhayl is said to have been sufficiently known before 803 to have been present at the symposium on love described by al-Masʿudī. Bishr is said to have been imprisoned for Shīʿite sympathies during the reign of Hārūn ar-Rashīd (786–809), and he is also said to have had Muʿammar as a teacher. It would therefore appear that Muʿtazilite discussions began some time before 800, though it may have been the latter part of the reign of al-Ma'mūn before the more important developments took place. It must be remembered that the period from 809 to 819, when al-Ma'mūn entered Baghdad as caliph, was a very troubled one, though we have no means of knowing whether theology was adversely affected.

Before saying anything about the detailed views of these "founding fathers" of the Mu'tazilites, it will be well to look at what preceded this outburst of theology. A frequently repeated story of the origin of the name "Mu'tazila" connects it with the discussion that took place in the circle of al-Ḥasan al-Baṣrī. Once when al-Ḥasan was asked his view on the dispute between the Murji'ites, who said the grave sinner was a believer, and most of the Khārijites, who said the grave sinner was an unbeliever, a man interrupted before al-Ḥasan could reply and asserted that the grave sinner was in an "intermediate position". This man, Wāṣil ibn-'Aṭā', then withdrew from the circle, and al-Ḥasan remarked, "He has withdrawn (*i'tazala*) from us"; from this remark he and his party were called the Mu'tazila (the corresponding participial form). Unfortunately this is not the only account of the origin of the Mu'tazila. A similar story is told of al-Ḥasan's pupil Qatāda and another man 'Amr ibn-'Ubayd; and this latter man is often referred to as the founder of the Mu'tazila. The word, however, has other applications; it can be applied to recluses, and to neutrals who hold aloof from fighting. In any case there is nothing to suggest that Wāṣil or 'Amr had any of the interest in Greek philosophical conceptions which was the distinctive feature of the great Mu'tazilites; at most they can have been forerunners in holding the "intermediate position" and similar points with an immediate practical bearing.

A suggestion about the political attitude of the Muʿtazilites, put forward by the Swedish scholar H. S. Nyberg, has so far neither been enthusiastically welcomed nor decisively rejected.[8] It is that during the later Umayyad period Wāṣil and his followers were actively working for the ʿAbbāsid cause, and indeed that "the theology of Wāṣil and the original Muʿtazila was the official theology of the ʿAbbāsid movement". Apart from certain considerations of a general kind the chief argument for this hypothesis consists of some mysterious verses about sending out emissaries. Against the hypothesis is its failure to explain such a matter as the imprisonment of Bishr ibn-al-Muʿtamir and the relation of Wāṣil's theology to that of the ʿAbbāsid military leader Abū-Muslim.

The most serious criticism, however, is that this hypothesis tends to accept the accounts of the origins of the Muʿtazilites at their face value, whereas there are grounds for thinking they are later fabrications.[9] On the basis, then, of the unauthentic character of the usual accounts of the origins of the Muʿtazilites, some such view as the following has to be put forward. The real origin of the distinctive Muʿtazilite position, combining certain Islamic dogmas with Greek philosophical conceptions, was in the discussions at Basra towards the end of the eighth century. Naturally there was opposition, and among the taunts hurled at those who were trying to make use of Greek philosophy was one to the effect that they were followers of a man called JAHM. Why Jahm had such a bad reputation is not clear; what is clear is that an important section of the later Sunnites (the Ḥanbalites) used the term "Jahmite" roughly for all who were Muʿtazilites in the wider sense of using rational methods in theology. To avoid this charge those who accepted the five points (the Muʿtazilites in the strict sense) looked around for some more reputable figure whom they could claim as ancestor. Bishr ibn-al-Muʿtamir, as we know from verses ascribed to him which are almost certainly authentic, claimed to be a follower of ʿAmr ibn-ʿUbayd; others preferred Wāṣil ibn-ʿAṭāʾ. This difference may reflect some doctrinal differences within the Muʿtazilites. It may well be that in respect of political attitude the Muʿtazilites of the ninth century were close to ʿAmr and Wāṣil. Eventually, whether because Wāṣil was felt to be a better figure-head or because most Muʿtazilites preferred his views, he came to be regarded as the original founder of Muʿtazilism.

Can anything be said about this political attitude? If the Umayyad period is left aside, attention may be concentrated on Abū-ʾl-Hudhayl and his contemporaries, about whose views something is known. It is also known that towards the end of the reign of al-Maʾmūn important positions in the administration, including that of chief qāḍī, or judge, were given to men of Muʿtazilite sympathies. About the same time there began the Miḥna or "Inquisition" in which the chief officials in each province were required to make public profession of the doctrine that the Qurʾān was created—a Muʿtazilite doctrine. This was not a purely theological question, of course; the government was trying to get broader support for its policies by gaining the favour of the moderate Shīʿites; and the abandonment of this whole line of policy about 849 under al-Mutawakkil probably indicates primarily that it had not received the measure of support it hoped for. After this point the Muʿtazilites ceased to have political importance.

Their political attitude during the heyday of their influence may be described as aiming at broadening the support for the existing regime by compromise and by the balance of opposing interests. Something of this kind would be suggested by the mere fact of their alliance with the caliphs, since the ruler of such an empire as the Islamic must constantly have such an aim—witness the attempts of the Byzantine emperors to remove tensions between opposing Christian parties by a policy of theological compromise. A policy of compromise is also suggested by the fundamental Muʿtazilite doctrine of the "intermediate position"; while in the conflict between Sunnites and Shīʿites—or "constitutionalist" and "autocratic" blocs—they had views to please both sides: the doctrine of the createdness of the Qur'ān to please the Shīʿites (and partly undermine the position of the ulema), and only a modified recognition of ʿAlī to please the Sunnites. Like similar theological compromises among the Byzantines this one soon showed its unsatisfactory character. The Shīʿites objected to it because ʿAlī's "designation" as heir was not accepted; and the Sunnites disliked it because the doctrine of the createdness of the Qur'ān seemed to be the first step towards abandoning the Islamic (and charismatic) character of the community.

The first of the five points of the Muʿtazilites was that of "unity" or rather "assertion of unity" (*taw'ḥīd*), since the Arabic word means literally "the making one". This implied for them much more than the mere assertion that God was one and that there were not many gods. The Muslims were accustomed to say that God had ninety-nine "beautiful names", most of which are mentioned in the Qur'ān; seven of them received special attention from the theologians: the Knowing (or Omniscient), the Powerful (or Almighty), the Willing, the Living, the Hearing, the Seeing, the Speaking. Some theologians held that God had certain attributes (*ṣifāt*) corresponding to these names, namely, Knowledge, Power, Will, etc. To the Muʿtazilites, however, this seemed to be introducing an element of multiplicity into the unity of the divine nature or essence (*nafs*, *dhāt*), and in insisting on "unity" they were asserting that these attributes had no sort of independent or hypostatic existence, but were merged in the unity of God's being. In so far as God knew, he knew by himself or his essence, and not by any hypostatic Knowledge.

This discussion of the attributes seems to have developed out of the discussions about the Qur'ān. These may have begun before 750, but it is more likely that the Qur'ān only became a subject of vigorous argument towards the end of that century. The Muslims had always believed both that the Qur'ān was the Word of God and that it had appeared at a particular point in time, namely, when it was revealed to Muḥammad. Why anyone should want to insist either that it was created or that it was uncreated is not obvious. The question at issue was doubtless its status—was it the Word of God or not?—for this had practical implications. These have already been indicated in what was said about the "Inquisition" begun by al-Ma'mūn. A governmental attempt to reduce the status of the Qur'ān would be met by the insistence that it was the Speech of God and therefore eternal; while this insistence would call forth the contrary assertion that, since it had appeared at a point in time, it must be created. Arguments were developed on both sides with great subtlety, and the range of topics included in the discussion became ever wider.

Some examples of the arguments used will be illuminating. From a Qur'ānic verse (43.3/2) which runs "We have made it (*ja'alnā-hu*) an Arabic Qur'ān" it was argued that this "making" implies creating. Other verses were taken to imply that the Qur'ān was produced after something else; for example, "we shall tell thee tidings of what has preceded" (20.99), where the "tidings" are presumably part of the Qur'ān. On the other side one of the most ingenious arguments was from the passages, of which there are several, where a speech is addressed to Moses such as "I am thy Lord". Then it is argued that, if this is created, a created thing must have said to Moses "I am thy Lord" and Moses must have been guilty of idolatry in accepting this created thing as his Lord.

From arguments of this kind, which are often only verbal juggling, the discussion led on to deeper questions. The Muʿtazilites tried to baffle those who held that the Qur'ān was the uncreated Speech of God by asking about their own "utterance" (*lafẓ*) of the Qur'ān. When a Muslim recites the Qur'ān, his reciting of it is surely not uncreated. This puzzle rests of course on the special nature of speech. Indeed the whole discussion may be said to turn on the difference between the relation of speech to the speaker and the thing made or created to its maker or creator; speech is an expression of the character of the speaker to a much greater extent than the thing made is an expression of the character of its maker; indeed speech is in a sense one with the speaker, whereas the thing made is separate from its maker. At an even deeper level the discussion may be said to turn on how it is possible for the eternal to be manifested in time.

The conception of the Word or Speech of God as eternal is one of several points which have suggested to European scholars that the development of Islamic theology was largely influenced by Christian theology.[10] In this case there is the obvious comparison with Jesus as the eternal Word of God. The parallel, however, is not quite so close as it appears to be. The Arabic word applied to the Qur'ān is *kalām*, which is properly "speech", whereas there is a Qur'ānic verse (3.45/40) which speaks of Jesus as "a word" (*kalima*) from God. Even if the similarity were closer than this, it does not necessarily follow that there was any direct influence. Islamic theology is now seen to have been brought about by inner tensions. It is thus not to be supposed that Muslim theologians copied Christian conceptions simply for the sake of copying. What is possible is that, having some awareness of Christian conceptions, they found among them items which were useful to them in maintaining their position against Islamic rivals. This awareness might come about in two ways. There were many Christians who had become Muslims without completely forgetting their Christian ideas; some may have become theologians, or at least talked with theologians. Also a number of religious discussions between Muslims and Christians are known to have taken place. It is only in this indirect way by providing suitable materials or lines of argument that Christian or any other extraneous thought can have influenced Islamic theology. What in the first place made men want to argue came entirely from within Islam.

The transition from discussions about the Speech of God to general discussions about the attributes is an easy one. Those who say that the Qur'ān is eternal seem to their opponents to be saying that there are two eternal beings, God and the Qur'ān. One of the ways in which they tried to escape from this conclusion was by asserting that the Qur'ān was God's knowledge or part of his knowledge. They could then say to the opponents, "Is it possible for God to exist and his Knowledge not to exist?" If it was conceded that his Knowledge existed eternally, then the Qur'ān also existed eternally. The Mu'tazilites avoided this denial of one of their main doctrines by holding that God had no such hypostatic Knowledge in any way distinct from himself. They then applied this view to the other attributes.

The second of the five points which the Mu'tazilites regarded as defining their position was that of justice or righteousness (*'adl*). Indeed they liked to speak of themselves as "the people of unity and justice". In respect of their insistence on justice the Muʿtazilites may be regarded as heirs of the Khārijites. In practice this meant that they believed in man's responsibility for his acts or the freedom of the human will. They were thus also heirs of that section of the "general religious movement" which believed in thefreedom of the will and was called Qadarite by its opponents. The general conception of the freedom of the will was accepted by the Muʿtazilites, and the arguments tended to be about subordinate questions.

The central concern in this sphere is the relation of God to man's ultimate destiny—Paradise (Heaven) or Hell. By insisting on human freedom and responsibility the Muʿtazilites made man's ultimate destiny depend on himself. The basic thought was that God in revelation showed man what he ought to do to attain Paradise, and then left it to man himself to do it or not to do it. This gave a tidy rational scheme with Paradise as the reward for obedience and Hell as the punishment for disobedience. It is presupposed that God is somehow bound to give reward and punishment in this way. In due course, however, complications appeared. What about children? If they had not committed any sins, should they not go to Paradise? But, if they went to Paradise, they had not earned it by their obedience, and was that fair to others?

In this connection a reference to the story of the three brothers is not amiss. Though it is usually told to explain al-Ashʿarī's abandonment of the Muʿtazilites, it seems rather to contain a criticism of the Muʿtazilites of Baghdad by those of Basra. There were once three brothers, one good, one wicked, and one who died as a child; the first is in Paradise, the second in Hell, and the third in Limbo. The third is depicted as complaining that by being made to die early he has been given no chance to merit Paradise by his obedience—the commands and prohibitions of Islam were not applicable to children below a certain age, and so these could not be held either to obey or to disobey. He was given the reply that God caused him to die early because he foresaw that, if he grew up, he would be thoroughly wicked. Upon this the second brother asked why he also had not been made to die young before he committed the sins which brought him to Hell. To this, of course, there was no answer. The whole story is a critique of certain Muʿtazilites who held that God is bound to do what is best for men. The matter has further ramifications, too —the unmerited sufferings of children and the sufferings of animals, the latter perhaps introduced as the result of contact with Indian Brahmins.

The remaining three of the five points, though used to fix the Muʿtazilite position, hardly appeared in the theological discussions. In the second half of the first volume of the *Maqālāt* al-Ashʿarī devotes seventy-two pages to recording the various opinions of Muʿtazilites with respect to the first point, thirty-nine with respect to the second, and only thirteen with respect to the remaining three. The third point is "the promise and the threat" (*al-waʿd wa-'l-waʿīd*), or Paradise and Hell: the theological points discussed follow on the discussions between the Murji'ites and the Khārijites: what is faith? what is the difference between grave and slight sins, and ultimately between good and evil? from what kind of men can Traditions be accepted? The fourth point is the mainly political one of the "intermediate position" (*al-manzila bayn al-manzilatayn*). The fifth is "commanding the good and forbidding the evil" (*al-amr bi-'l-maʿrūf wa-'n-nahy ʿan al-munkar*), that is, interfering publicly to maintain the observance of the Sharīʿa; this again is mainly political, and may even justify revolt.

Enough is known about the distinctive views of the leading Muʿtazilites to make it possible to give an account of their individual positions, but to attempt this would be out of place in the present survey. It seems clear that the man who did most to establish the general Muʿtazilite position was ABŪ-'L-HUDHAYL, also known as al-ʿAllāf, who is reckoned the founder of Muʿtazilite theology in Basra. He madeconsiderable use of the Aristotelian conceptions of substance and accident, perhaps derived from Ḍirār; but in accordance with the atomism which came to dominate Islamic theology he regarded the accidents as lasting each for only a single (atomic) moment. Also at Basra was AN-NAẒẒĀM, a follower of Abū-'l-Hudhayl but probably not much younger; he showed much initiative in pioneering the application of Greek conceptions to Islamic themes, even though the lines he opened up were not always eventually followed.[11] Muʿammar (or Maʿmar), probably somewhat earlier, was certainly influential, but remains mysterious.

The Muʿtazilites of Bagdad regarded BISHR IBN-AL-MUʿTAMIR as their founder. Among the doctrines specially associated with him is that of "generated effects" (*tawallud*), which raised the problem of how far a man was responsible for his acts—a problem which doubtless led on to the acceptance by the Ashʿarites of the doctrine of "acquisition".[12] A little later there was a notable triad at Baghdad, AL-ISKĀFĪ (d. 854) and the two JAʿFARS, Jaʿfar ibn-Ḥarb (d. 850) and Jaʿfar ibn-al-Mubashshir (d. 848). It was about the time when they were active that the doctrine that God must do what is best (*aṣlaḥ*) for men became popular in Baghdad. The story of the three brothers mentioned above was apparently intended as criticism of this doctrine. This criticism was made in the school of Basra, whose head at the close of the ninth century was AL-JUBBĀ'Ī (850–915), the teacher of al-Ashʿarī. Al-Jubbā'ī was succeeded by his son ABŪ-HĀSHIM (d. 933) who made less than his father of the inexplicable aspect of "uncovenanted goodness" (*tafaḍḍul*) in God's dealings with men, and was also responsible for a subtle refinement of the doctrine of the divine attributes known as the doctrine of "states" (*aḥwāl*).

The Muʿtazilites continued after this for some time, but mainly as a school of academic theologians with practically no popular following. Even as theologians they do not appear to have made any significant contributions to the development of their subject. The last important name among the theologians proper is the chief qāḍī ʿABD-AL-JABBĀR (d. 1025), but the philologist and Qur'ān-commentator AZ-ZAMAKHSHARI (d. 1144) had Muʿtazilite leanings, being connected with a group in the remote region of Khwarizm (south of the Aral sea). Such a decline was only natural after the central Muʿtazilite position had ceased to be relevant to contemporary life and had been decided against by the community as a whole. This decline, however, does not cancel out the great contribution made by the Muʿtazilites to the intellectual life of Islam in that they were the chief founders of the discipline of speculative or philosophical theology.

BIBLIOGRAPHY

H. S. NYBERG, arts. "Muʿtazila", "al-Naẓẓām", in *EI(S)*; also edition with Arabic introduction of al-Khayyāṭ, *Kitāb al-Intiṣār*, Cairo, 1925 (French translation by A. N. Nader, Beirut, 1957.) The latter is an important early source.

Albert N. NADER, *Le Système philosophique des Muʿtazila*, Beirut, 1956 (also in Arabic); presents Muʿtazilite theology as a system, without considering historical development.

W. Montgomery Watt, "The Political Attitudes of the Muʿtazilah", *Journal of the Royal Asiatic Society*, 1963, 38-57; *Free Will and Predestination*, 61-92; also "Early Discussions about the Qur'ān", *Muslim World*, xl (1950), 27-40, 96-105.

CHAPTER 8

THE CONSOLIDATION OF SUNNISM

THOUGH what may be called the consolidation of the Sunnite position in Islam does not belong, strictly speaking, to the history of Islamic theology, it forms an essential part of the background. In the latter half of the Umayyad period there took shape what has here been called the "general religious movement". This included men whose primary interests were in theology or in mysticism and asceticism, but the main focus of interest was probably law. From this aspect the movement may be described as the "ancient schools" of law. Large sections of the general movement supported the ʿAbbāsid cause, and when the ʿAbbāsids came to power they gave some recognition to the nascent discipline of Islamic law in the establishment of their judicial system. At the same time they tried to curb the individualism of the various local schools, each of which went its own way and disagreed with the others on many points of detail. The ʿAbbāsid government, therefore, brought pressure to bear on the "schools" to achieve some measure of unity and agreement. One of the results of this pressure was to encourage the movement for giving special status to Traditions from the Prophet. Hitherto it had been customary for men to say, "The teaching of our school is ..."; or they might support this by reference to a remark by some distinguished member of the school in the past. Eventually some schools began to justify some of their teachings by referring to an anecdote about something Muḥammad had said or done. As a result of the work of ash-Shāfi'ī (767–820) the methodological superiority of this justification of juristic principles was universally recognized, and all the schools began to claim that their teachings were in accordance with Qur'ān and Tradition.

The growth of interest in Traditions (in this technical sense of anecdotes about Muḥammad) may not be entirely due to the needs of jurisprudence. Indeed there must have been a core of genuine biographical material.[13] It is also clear, however, that authentic sayings of Muḥammad were slightly altered in order to make a legal point, while much of the inherited wisdom of the Middle East was fathered on to him, including a recognizable version of the Christian Paternoster. It was not long before Muslim scholars recognized what was happening, and began to take precautions against it. The basic method was to require that each Tradition should be supported by an *isnād* or "chain of authorities". Thus the narrator of a Tradition would say: "I heard this from A, and he said that he heard it from B, and he said that he heard it from C, who said he was present when Muḥammad made the remark". This leads to a scrutiny of the biographical aspect of the chain of authorities, and to a general interest in biography, which led to large numbers of biographical dictionaries. It is important to know that dates make it possible for each authority to have actually heard the anecdote from his predecessor, and for the earliest to have seen and known Muḥammad (and so to be technically a "Companion"). The critic must also consider whether all the links in the chain were men of sound views; people who belonged to or sympathized with a heretical sect were not acceptable as transmitters, and their presence in a chain reduced the value of the Tradition. The inclusion of a man who was known to have been careless and inexact in his methods also "weakened" a Tradition.

Unfortunately in a largely oral culture it is difficult, once a story has been spread, to suppress it; all that can be done is to modify it, or reinterpret it, or to give wide currency to a superior alternative story with allegedly better support. Consequently it became usual to classify Traditions and transmitters in various grades. Traditions might be described as "weak" or "worthless", but were not said to be outright falsehoods. Most important, of course, were the "sound" Traditions; and the middle of the ninth century saw great collections of these made for legal purposes. The chief were those of AL-BUKHĀRĪ (d. 870) and MUSLIM (d. 875). Others, arranged sometimes according to different plans, gave additional anecdotes, and also similar anecdotes with different authority-chains. Eventually the two mentioned and four others (produced within the following forty years) came to be recognized as canonical.

European and American scholars, by insisting that the critique of Traditions by medieval Muslim scholars accepted as "sound" much that could not be historically authentic, have obscured the positive achievement of the Traditionists of the ninth century. This was no less than the consolidation of Sunnism. Up to this point it had been possible to modify genuine sayings of Muḥammad or to invent new ones *and to have these widely accepted.* With the growth and general acceptance of a definite canon this was no longer possible to the same extent. Traditions might indeed still be invented, but it was no longer easy to have them accepted and used to justify some change in the life of the community. Thus the period just before the formation of the canon became the classical age of Islam in the sense that it was the model to which later generations looked back and tried to conform even when circumstances forced changes upon them. Because they were ostensibly following the example of Muhammad, Muslims themselves may not have realized just what they were doing. They were in fact following the early ninth century's conception of the example of Muḥammad, and therefore the early ninth century's values.

The establishment of the canon of "sound" Tradition may be looked at also in other perspectives. For one thing it belongs to the struggle between Shī'ism and Sunnism. The Sunnite religious and political attitude was now supported by a tolerably coherent body of doctrine and was therefore strengthened *vis-à-vis* its rival. The change of policy that was decided on early in the reign of al-Mutawakkil (847–61) is doubtless somehow linked with the consolidation of Sunnism—probably neither simply as cause nor as effect but by a more complex relationship. Again the formation of the canon belongs to the history of the position of the Sunnite ulema in the caliphate. The existence of a discipline with a definite corpus of material fostered professionalism, for it became comparatively easy to say who were proficient in the discipline and who were not. Presumably the existence of the canon made it easier for the ulema to resist undue pressure from the government. Their position had been weakened by the "Inquisition" in respect of the createdness of the Qur'ān. The two points here mentioned may be regarded as gains, on the whole, for the community, but they were offset by losses, notably a decreased possibility of adaptation to changing circumstances.

The formation of the canon of "sound" Tradition is an indication of the growing strength of the Traditionist movement. The Traditionists were first and foremost men who specialized in the collection and transmission of Traditions; and more and more the study of Tradition became one of the academic disciplines ancillary to the study of jurisprudence, having among its practitioners men of many different shades of opinion. In the formative period before 850, however, the Traditionists were not so much specialists in Tradition as persons with a particular doctrinal standpoint. In the "general religious movement" of Umayyad times, out of which the Traditionist movement grew, many different opinions had been held; there had been upholders of the freedom of the human will and upholders of the doctrine of Murji'ism (that a grave sinner still belongs to the community), and a few among the Traditionists sympathized with these views. Gradually, however, the Traditionist movement settled down to a rejection of the extreme doctrines of free will and of Murji'ism and to the formulation of the great dogmas of Sunnism. There were also men of Shī'ite sympathies among the Traditionists at first; but in the ninth century Shī'ite insistence that 'Alī had been designated by Muḥammad as imām after himself forced them to regard most of the Companions as unreliable transmitters and to form their own corpus of Tradition, which often included one of the Shī'ite imāms in the authority-chain. Thus to the Traditionist movement are due not merely the canon of "sound" Tradition, but also the broad lines of Sunnite dogma.

One dogma about which much is heard is that of the uncreated and eternal character of the Qur'ān. Much has already been said about this in the account of the Mu'tazilites, and it remains only to look at it in the context of the Traditionist movement. When the "Inquisition" was established towards the end of the reign of al-Ma'mūn (813–33) and officials were required to state publicly that they held the Qur'ān to be created, most of those summoned to do so complied. Among those who refused, however, was AḤMAD IBN-ḤANBAL (780–855). He was imprisoned for about two years, from 833 to 835, and then set free. After 842 the prohibition on lecturing seems to have been removed, but apart from one attempt to start he refrained from giving lectures, perhaps because he realized it would endanger his life. When the Sunnites came into favour again under al-Mutawakkil, he was apparently too old to take up any active work. There is no reason to suppose that the stand made by Ibn-Ḥanbal on the uncreatedness of the Qur'ān had anything to do with the reversal of government policy. At most it can have shown the government the strength of popular feeling in Baghdad. Ibn-Ḥanbal's stand, however, may have focused attention on him within the Traditionist movement, so that an important section of what may be called the conservative wing of the movement came to be known as the Ḥanbalites.

The term "conservative" is here used to describe one side of a fierce debate which went on for many decades within the movement, and indeed continued in other forms for centuries. It was a debate about method, and it applied to both law and theology. In law the Ḥanafites, the adherents of the legal rite (or school) of Abū-Ḥanīfa, were specially noted for their readiness to employ what might roughly be called "reason" or "common sense" and to argue by analogy from one case to a slightly different one. Some Ḥanafites also became interested in the use of reason in doctrinal matters on similar lines to the Mu'tazilites. One man who was prominent in this respect was Bishr ibn-Ghiyāth al-Marīsī (d. 833), but, apart from the question of the use of reason, he adopted dogmatic positions which were eventually rejected by the main body of Sunnites (such as the createdness of the Qur'ān) and had little following among the Ḥanafites.

It must not be thought, however, that all the Ḥanafites were committed to rational methods in theology. There appears to have been a central body who, in step with other Sunnites, were working out the Sunnite dogmatic position. Different stages in the development of this are illustrated by the Hanafite creeds translated by A. J. Wensinck in *The Muslim Creed*; his commentary on them shows how they are linked up with Traditions. What he calls "Fiqh Akbar I" is simple, and might be from Abū-Ḥanīfa himself (d. 767). "The Testament of Abū-Ḥanīfa" contains the doctrine of the uncreated Qur'ān and other anti-Mu'tazilite doctrines, and must therefore be dated from about 820 to 840. "Fiqh Akbar II" has an article which mentions the attributes of God, and would appear to have been composed between 900 and 950. The creed of aṭ-Ṭaḥāwī (*c.* 850–933) is more "conservative" than the "Testament" and may date from about 890 to 910; it has an article against theological discussions. What is said about the attributes in "Fiqh Akbar II", on the other hand, makes it likely that some discussion had preceded.

All this is evidence that two processes must have been going on among the Ḥanafites. One is the elaboration of dogma, and this process is an important part of the elaboration of the central Sunnite dogmatic position. Yet it must be noted that there is a family resemblance in these Ḥanafite creeds, and certain slight differences between them and, for example, the creed of al-Ash'arī—an illustration is that he thinks faith increases and decreases and the Ḥanafites tend to deny this. These differences, too, are not unlike the differences between the much more "theological" formulations of the Ash'arite and Māturīdite schools. The second process is that of extending the use of rational methods of argument, but no details are known of how this came about. The Ḥanafite name parallel to that of al-Ash'arī is that of al-Māturīdī, who died in Samarqand in 944. Despite his importance, however, and the existence of a theological school bearing his name, practically nothing is known about the man himself or his immediate antecedents.

Titles of books have been preserved which show he attacked contemporary Muʿtazilites.

It was apparently also among the Hanafites that there developed another group of theologians engaged in defending a central Sunnite position against the Muʿtazilites and others. The founder was Ibn-Karrām (d. 869), and his followers continued to be a distinct sect or group among the Sunnites of Khurasan for two or three centuries. Various incidents involving Karrāmites are recorded by the historians, but little is known about their theological views beyond what is found in the heresiographers, since none of their theological works seem to have been preserved. Some of the Karrāmites became noted as mystics, however, and perhaps a fuller examination of the historical materials in connection with the mystical works would lead to a deeper understanding.[14] The existence of the group shows that the move towards philosophical theology was widespread.

The relation between legal rites and theological schools may be noticed. The four main Sunnite rites are the Ḥanafite, Mālikite, Shāfiʿite and Ḥanbalite, which are equally valid, though differing from one another on minor points. (The term "rite" is preferable to "school" since matters of practice and not only opinions are involved; every Sunnite belongs to one of the four rites and has his affairs judged according to it in the law-courts.) There is no logical reason why followers of one rite should tend to adopt one form of theological doctrine. Yet in the ʿAbbāsid period there is a tendency for Ḥanafites to be Māturīdites and for Mālikites and Shāfiʿites to be Ashʿarites, even if there are exceptions such as certain of the Karrāmites. In the case of the Ḥanbalites there is virtually complete identity between the legal rite and the theological school, perhaps because of their rejection of rational methods in theology. Certainly Aḥmad ibn-Ḥanbal became the most prominent upholder of the "conservative" viewpoint on this question. His rejection of rational and philosophical argument in matters of doctrine, however, was no mere obscurantism, and was not due to a failure to rise to the intellectual level of the Muʿtazilites. Some centuries later a distinguished Ḥanbalite Ibn-Taymiyya wrote a "Refutation of the Systematic Logicians" which showed complete mastery of the subject. This helps to show that the Ḥanbalite position was based on an awareness of the limitations of reason in this sphere, coupled with an understanding of the need to retain the concrete and "poetical" language of the Qur'ān and the Traditions. Reason likes to have an ordered system, but religious truth, Ibn-Ḥanbal felt, cannot be thus systematized. There were naïve anthropomorphists among the Traditionists, but he opposed these as vigorously as he opposed the Muʿtazilites; he insisted that the anthropomorphic expressions of the Qur'ān are to be understood "without stating the precise manner of their existence" (*bi-lā kayf*, literally "without how").[15] The strength of Ibn-Ḥanbal's feelings on this matter may be gauged by the fact that he broke off relations with a follower who attempted to refute the Muʿtazilites by their own methods of argument.

The late ninth and early tenth centuries constituted a period of advance in the movement of sufism or mysticism, and this had some repercussions on theology. It was inevitable that the sufis should have a dogmatic position, and should at various points prefer one or other of the usual theological schools. A long chapter in Louis Massignon's study of the sufi al-Ḥallāj (d. 922) is devoted to his dogmatic views. It seems clear, however, that there was no sufficiently coherent body of sufistic theological thought to provoke the main theological schools to reply. Massignon suggests that the discussion of apologetic miracles found from the time of al-Bāqillānī (d. 1013) onwards was triggered off by the claims of al-Ḥallāj. The group of sufis who came nearest being a school of dogmatic theology is that of the Sālimiyya, who came into existence shortly before 900 and can be traced for some two hundred and fifty years. Despite the study of them by Goldziher and Massignon they remain a bit obscure. One of the puzzles is that they seem to have provoked criticism only among Ḥanbalites.[16]

Bibliography

(See also the Bibliography to ch. 4.)

W. M. Patton, *Aḥmed b. Ḥanbal and the Miḥna*, Leiden, 1897; review of basic material.

Margaret Smith, *An Early Mystic of Baghdad*, London, 1935; J. van Ess, *Die Gedankenwelt des Ḥārit al-Muḥāsibī*, Bonn, 1961. Both deal with a friend of Ibn-Ḥanbal, and the first particularly lays most emphasis on mysticism.

James Robson, *An Introduction to the Science of Tradition* . . ., London, 1953; translation of an Arabic work which gives some idea of the methods of criticism employed by Muslim scholars.

CHAPTER 9

AL-ASH'ARI

THE movement towards a rational defence of the central dogmatic positions of Sunnism finds its climax—in the absence of fuller information about al-Māturīdī—in the "conversion" of AL-ASH'ARĪ (Abū-'l-Ḥasan 'Alī ibn-Ismā'īl). He was born at Basra in 873, and studied under the head of the Mu'tazilites there, al-Jubbā'ī. As a distinguished pupil he sometimes took the place of the master, and might conceivably have succeeded him, it is said. On the other hand, al-Jubbā'ī had a very intelligent son, Abū-Hāshim, who did in fact succeed him; and it may be that rivalry between this man and al-Ash'arī was a factor contributing to his abandonment of the Mu'tazilites, which took place about 912, shortly before the death of the master in 915. The positive side of this "conversion" was the acceptance of Sunnite dogma in its Ḥanbalite form; and for the rest of his life al-Ash'arī devoted himself to the intellectual defence of this position. He died in 935.

A theological motive for the change is suggested in some of the sources in the form of the story of the three brothers, as noted above. The proper interpretation of this matter would appear to be that there was growing dissatisfaction among the Mu'tazilites of Basra with the attempts to give a rational account of the variations in men's destinies. It looks as if al-Ash'arī, carrying his master's line of thought a little farther, came to the conclusion that revelation was superior to reason as a guide to life, and decided to attach himself to those who, quite explicitly, placed revelation in this place. In his works he professes himself to be a follower of Aḥmad ibn-Ḥanbal.

Besides the strictly theological motive al-Ashʿarī was presumably dissatisfied with the Muʿtazilite position because it was ceasing to be relevant to the contemporary situation. It has been suggested above that Muʿtazilism was essentially an attempt to work out a compromise that would in part overcome the cleavage between Sunnites and Shīʿites. The government abandoned the attempt to base itself on such a compromise about the middle of the ninth century, and became more definitely pro-Sunnite. In the following half-century the consolidation of Sunnism was achieved. At the same time the vagueness of the Rāfiḍites had been replaced by the much more definite Imāmite form of Shīʿism. Thus by 912 there had been a hardening of both Sunnism and Shīʿism, and it must have been clear to acute observers that the prospects of anything being achieved by the Muʿtazilite compromise were rapidly declining. The Muʿtazilites had in fact become a group of academic theologians who had retired to an ivory tower remote from the pressures and tensions of the times. Or, to put it in another way, the Greek ideas with which they played were not sufficiently Greek for the philosophers, yet sometimes were too far removed from the religion of the masses to be generally acceptable. The consolidation of Sunnism meant that a great body of people had accepted a fairly definite set of dogmas, and that there was no longer any hope of wide acceptance for doctrines like those of the Muʿtazilites which differed more than a little from these dogmas.

It is tolerably certain, then, that this situation had much to do with al-Ashʿarī's conversion, but it need not be supposed that he thought about it in such terms. His response to the situation may have been directed in the main by his unconscious mind. The accounts which have been preserved of a series of dreams he had are fully in accordance with the outlook of modern psychology, and there is no reason why they should not be authentic, apart from the slight variations. In these dreams, which occurred during the month of Ramaḍān (the month of fasting, comparable in some ways to the Christian Lent), the Prophet Muḥammad appeared three times to al-Ashʿarī. On the first occasion he told the theologian to support what was related from himself, that is, the Traditions. Al-Ashʿarī, dissatisfied with the rationalistic methods of the Muʿtazilites, did then turn to the Traditions, but occupied himself in interpreting them according to Muʿtazilite methods. When the Prophet appeared again a few days later, he asked how his injunction to support what had been related from himself had been obeyed, and on being informed simply repeated it. Another version of the story, however, says that al-Ashʿarī first studied the Traditions about seeing Muḥammad in dreams (since he doubted the reality of his experience), about intercession and about the vision of God in Paradise. Al-Ashʿarī is also reported to have said to Muḥammad that he doubted the vision of God with the eyes because it was contrary to reason, and to have received the reply that it was not the Traditions that were doubtful but the arguments of reason.

After the second dream, in all versions, he completely gave up rational methods, and confined himself to a study of Traditions and of commentaries on the Qur'ān. A few days later the Prophet appeared for the third time, and again asked how his instructions had been followed out. He was not altogether pleased, however, when he was told, and said: "I did not tell you to give up rational arguments, but to support the true Traditions". On the basis of this conception al-Ashʿarī worked out his new theological position which may be described as the support of revelation by reason. This implies of course a subordination of reason. Such an attitude is in line with the growing awareness among the Mu'tazilites of Basra of the inadequacy of rational conceptions. The Traditions selected for study deal with subjects relevant to this point, for the Prophet's intercession for sinners was a corrective of strict justice, and the vision of God with the eyes in the next world was complementary to the limitations of our rational conceptions of him in this.

The reader who now turns to translations of the works of al-Ash'arī may at first find it difficult to discern any traces of "rational method" in them. They mostly consist of arguments from Qur'ānic verses and Traditions. Yet even here a knowledge of the writings of men in the strict Ḥanbalite tradition shows that al-Ash'arī really argues about these matters to a far greater extent. In addition other arguments are based on points of observation or of common knowledge, or on what the Muslims are agreed about. Despite appearances, then, al-Ash'arī really introduced rational arguments; and this little piece of leaven quickly spread through the lump of Islamic theology.

Some idea may be gained of the theological position of al-Ash'arī by considering under four heads his differences from the Mu'tazilites. This will also reveal his affinity to Aḥmad ibn-Ḥanbal. Firstly, he held that the Qur'ān was uncreated and was the very Speech of God, and that it, like his other attributes, was eternal and in some sense distinct from his essence. He does not here appear to have added anything of note to the doctrine of Aḥmad ibn-Ḥanbal, though there is greater subtlety in his arguments. Something similar may be said about the second point, the anthropomorphic expressions in the Qur'ān. The Mu'tazilites had held, for example, that where the Qur'ān speaks about God's "hand" what is meant is his "grace"; this could be supported by metaphorical usages of the word "hand" in Arabic, comparable to the English "lend a hand". On such points al-Ash'arī opposed the Mu'tazilites, and insisted that such Qur'ānic phrases must simply be accepted "without specifying how". Under the third head come various eschatological matters, which al-Ash'arī insisted must be taken as they stand and not explained as metaphors. Most discussion was devoted to the vision of God in Paradise by the faithful. Here the tendency of the Mu'tazilites was to say that this meant they would know him in their hearts (the heart being the seat of knowledge); but al-Ash'arī argued forcibly that the phrase "looking to their Lord" could mean only looking in the normal sense. He understood the vision of course "without specifying how", and would have rejected the attribution to God of anything resembling corporeality.

The fourth point, the rejection of the Mu'tazilite doctrine of free will, may be treated at greater length. On the human side there is the mysterious conception of "acquisition" (*kasb*, *iktisāb*). The common formula was that God creates the acts of a man, and that the man "acquires" them. Al-Ash'arī is often said to have invented the conception of "acquisition", which became so distinctive a mark of his followers that there was a saying: "more obscure than the 'acquisition' of the Ash'arites". It appears, however, that it was used a century before him by Abū-'l-Hudhayl's predecessor at Basra, Ḍirār ibn-'Amr. Indeed, although al-Ash'arī discussed various matters in terms of "acquisition", he does not seem to have been specially interested in the idea. "Acquisition" is best understood as a convenient name for the relation of a man to his act, where the omnipotence of God is taken seriously. It is a relation sufficient to make a man genuinely responsible for the act. Some other word such as "appropriation" might be more comprehensible in English, but "acquisition" is closer to the normal meaning of the Arabic word.[17]

It may help the modern reader to appreciate the formula of "creation by God and 'acquisition' by man" if he regards the aspect of creation as the influence of all the natural forces involved. These include those belonging to the agent's body as an entity obeying physical and chemical laws. Thus the shooting of an arrow presupposes and involves a man's ability to stand or kneel and to flex his arm muscles, and also the normal behaviour of the materials of the bow, of the air and of the object hit. Gravity and light also play a part. In Muslim eyes all this is the province of God as creator; man's share in the act, or his "acquisition" of it, is whatever is left. Even from a modern scientific viewpoint man does not make or bring into existence any of the objects or forces involved, though in daily life the ordinary man or woman takes them for granted; when everything of this sort has been set aside as not belonging to the essential human act, what is left—the inner decision—is very little.

By the time of al-Ashʿarī the field of discussion had been extended, and one of the points now to the fore was man's power or capacity to perform an act. Some thought of man's physical power; but most saw that the critical question was about volition—the power to initiate a chain of natural happenings. The Muʿtazilites held that this power to will an act must be a power to will either the act or its opposite—either obedience to a command or disobedience—and that it must also (according to their atomistic conceptions) exist in the moment before the act. Al-Ashʿarī denied this, and argued for an alternative—the power to act is a power to do only the act, not the opposite, and it exists only in the moment of acting, neither before nor afterwards (again in accordance with atomistic conceptions); moreover it is created by God. This gives little scope to man. He can hardly be said to initiate; he does little more than "accept as his" what God does through him. It is little wonder that even Sunnite critics of Ashʿarism like the Māturīdites called this a doctrine of "compulsion" (*jabr*). Yet al-Ashʿārī considered that it gave man sufficient responsibility for him to be justly punished or rewarded at the Last Judgement. As all who are "twice-born" tend to do, he makes much of what is done in him and relegates his own activity to an inferior place. Strange as the Ashʿarite doctrine is at first sight, it is not far removed from the Pauline conception: "work out your own salvation with fear and trembling; for it is God who worketh in you both to will and to do of his good pleasure" (Philippians, 2.12 f.), that is, God effects both the willing and the doing of what is for his chosen purpose.

Al-Ashʿarī's primary concern is to maintain God's omnipotence. For him this is something in the present, and is quite distinct from the old Arabian conception, which also found a home in Islam, that there had been an impersonal predestination and predetermination of men's lives in the distant past. There is a certain profundity in the answers al-Ashʿarī gives to the difficulties about God creating evil. Since God is omnipotent he must be the creator of all that is evil; but al-Ashʿarī insisted that the relationship of creation is not such that evil is attributed to God in the same way as to an evildoer. This is similar to God's creation of movement in one of his creatures; God is not, because of this creation of movement, described as moving. Al-Ashʿarī also produces instances where a man's act of will may contribute to bringing about an evil act or situation and yet the man is in no way an evildoer. In the Qur'ānic story of Joseph, for example, when he repeatedly refused the solicitations of his master's wife and she threatened him with imprisonment, he called out, "My Lord, I prefer the prison to that to which they invite me". By thus striving to serve God and avoid sin Joseph in a sense willed his own imprisonment; and that imprisonment was unjust and therefore evil. Thus he brought about a state of affairs that was evil, and yet he was not in any way sinful because of it. The real conclusion is that the relationship of human wills cannot be understood by physical analogies. Al-Ash'arī does not formulate it like this, of course; but is content to conclude that it is possible for God to create evil or to will folly without being an evildoer or foolish.

Such are some of the positions and arguments of al-Ash'arī. His work marks the recession of the first wave of Hellenism. Greek thought had been avidly seized upon by a small section of the more educated Muslims. Some, especially those hostile to the nascent Sunnism, committed themselves entirely to the guidance of reason as that was understood in Greek philosophy, and gave no more than lip service to Islamic religion. More important was the attempt of the Mu'tazilites and others to effect a fusion of Islamic dogma and the Greek intellectual tradition. Though the first enthusiasts may have made too great concessions to the Greek outlook, they undoubtedly raised the level of intellectual life among Muslims. Al-Ash'arī's service was to discern a way of assimilating most of the basic elements of Greek thought without compromising any of the central dogmas of Sunnite Islam. Thus Islam emerged from the first wave of Hellenism still recognizably itself, though changed in certain respects. Were these changes only peripheral, or did they ultimately come to influence the central core? This question is perhaps unanswerable, but it is worth keeping in mind.

Bibliography

R. C. McCarthy, *The Theology of al-Ash'ari*, Beirut, 1953; translation of some important works, with notes, and also certain texts.

Walter C. Klein, *Al-Aš'arī's Al-Ibānah*, New Haven, 1940; translation of one work with introduction and notes; less important than the above. Reviewed by William Thomson in *The Muslim World*, xxxii (1942), 242-60.

Joseph Schacht in *Studia Islamica*, i. 23-42, "New Sources for the History of Muhammedan Theology"; also speaks of al-Māturīdī.

W. Montgomery Watt, "The Origin of the Islamic Doctrine of Acquisition", *Journal of the Royal Asiatic Society*, 1943, 234-47; also *Free Will and Predestination*, 135-64.

Part Three

THE SECOND WAVE OF HELLENISM
950–1258

THE HISTORICAL BACKGROUND

POLITICALLY the period from 950 to 1258 is one of confusion and disintegration. The ʿAbbāsid caliphs had lost most of their power and had become little more than the ceremonial heads of a group of states often not at peace with one another. Indeed, even the nominal suzerainty of the caliphs was not always recognized. In 969 the Fāṭimid dynasty established itself in Egypt with its capital in the new city of Cairo; it sent emissaries into the Asiatic parts of the Islamic world preaching a form of Ismāʿīlite Shīʿism and aiming at the overthrow of the existing regimes. Since 945 Baghdad and the caliph himself had been controlled by the Buwayhid sultans, who were Shīʿites. Though Shīʿism seemed to be thus in the ascendant, Sunnism was deeply rooted in the common people, and such pressure as the governments were able to bear had little permanent effect on the religious outlook of ordinary men.

The eleventh century saw a political revival of Sunnism. An important state was created by Maḥmūd of Ghazna (998–1030) and his successors, first in Persia, then in Transoxiana, Central Asia and North-west India. Maḥmūd, who was of Turkish origin, put himself forward as a champion of Sunnism and supporter of the caliph. Shortly afterwards another Turkish dynasty replaced the Ghaznavids in their northern and western dominions, and eventually in 1055 occupied Baghdad and replaced the Buwayhids whose grasp for some time had been very weak. This dynasty was the Seljūqs, and their rule may be reckoned as lasting about a century, though in the latter half of that period they were much weaker than in the first half. They also did much to support and strengthen Sunnism.

It was about this time that the Crusaders from Europe appeared, capturing Antioch in 1098 and Jerusalem in 1099. Though the Crusaders maintained a foothold in Syria and Palestine for about a century and a half, to the Muslims in general they were never much more than a frontier incident. Such success as they had was possible because of the divided condition of this part of the Muslim world; and in the total pattern they were merely one of half a dozen groups contending for power. Compared with the intellectual impact of the Crusades on Christendom, that on the Islamic world was negligible. Out of the struggle with the Crusaders came the break-down of the Fāṭimids in Egypt, and their replacement by the Ayyūbids under Saladin (Ṣalāḥ-ad-Dīn, *regnabat* 1169–1193). This, the only other notable dynasty of the period, was also Sunnite.

The end of the period came about through the invasion of the Mongols, a series of events whose frightsomeness is no less than that of the bombing of Hiroshima. They came from the Asian steppes into Persia under Chingiz Khan (*regnabat* 1175–1227), who had established his rule over a vast area. In 1258 the Mongol commander in the Middle East, Hulagu, captured Baghdad and killed the last of the true 'Abbāsid caliphs. The Mongols did not establish a state here, but soon retired to Central Asia, leaving confusion behind except in Egypt (under the Mamlūks).

CHAPTER 10

THE FLOWERING OF PHILOSOPHY

PHILOSOPHY continued to be cultivated during the tenth century in small groups. The Muslim students of the subject were far from being fanatical adherents of Islam, and, in philosophical discussions and even in the work of teaching, Muslims and Christians seem to have associated on equal terms. There was, of course, still a tendency for philosophy to be connected with medicine. In particular we hear of a coterie in Baghdad towards the end of the tenth century, which met in the house of ABŪ-SULAYMĀN AL-MANṬIQĪ ("the logician") as-Sijistānī (d. after 1001). Unlike most philosophers Abū-Sulaymān seems to have held no official position, though he was in favour at the Buwayhid court. Some of the discussions in his house have been recorded by his younger friend ABŪ-ḤAYYĀN AT-TAW'ḤĪDĪ (d. after 1010) who was an important literary figure, though he earned his livelihood as a secretary to viziers and other court-officials in Baghdad and the provinces.[1]

Another man who deserves to be mentioned is MISKAWAYH (or Ibn-Miskawayh) (d. 1030). He was a Persian and served as secretary to members of the Buwayhid reigning family and their viziers. He is best known for a lengthy universal history, of which the concluding part has been translated into English as *The Eclipse of the 'Abbāsid Caliphate*.[2] Among his other extant works is a book of philosophical theology, dealing with the being of God, the being of the soul and the nature of prophethood. It is not an important book in the intellectual history of Islam, but it is an interesting example of how thinkers who were primarily philosophers nevertheless accepted a framework of Islamic conceptions; the last section of this book for example, explains in terms of a philosophical account of the soul how prophethood is possible.[3] Philosophically, however, his most influential work is undoubtedly his *Correction of Morals*,[4] which is an exposition of a complete system of morals on a mainly Platonic basis. This book was used by al-Ghazālī and many other later writers.

Philosophy must have been cultivated at many centres in the Islamic world. By chance we hear of men versed in the philosophical sciences at a small town near the south coast of the Caspian Sea. At least it was a man from this town who gave the first instruction in philosophy to a boy who later became in the opinion of many the greatest of all the philosophers writing in Arabic. This was AVICENNA, or Abū-ʿAlī ibn-Sīnā (980–1037). He was mainly of Persian stock, it would seem, but may also have had Turkish blood. He grew up in Bukhara, and began his education by memorizing the Qur'ān and Arabic poetry, before passing on to jurisprudence. He was possibly only about fourteen when the visiting scholar mentioned above introduced him to Aristotelian logic, and found to his surprise that the boy soon had a better grasp of the subject than his teacher. With an insatiable thirst for knowledge Avicenna then devoured all the scientific and philosophical books he could get hold of. He studied medicine, apparently by himself, and obtained so thorough a theoretical grasp that practising physicians came to read medical books under his guidance. According to the autobiographical fragment from which we derive this information all this happened before he was seventeen; and he also tested out and increased his medical knowledge by treating patients.

In this course of omnivorous study the one subject

which gave him trouble was metaphysics. He says he had read over Aristotle's *Metaphysica* forty times and had the text by heart, and yet he was baffled by it, until he chanced to come on a little book by al-Fārābī which brought him full illumination. This anecdote indicates that it was the direct influence of the older Islamic philosopher which led him to adopt so similar a general position in philosophy. For the next year or so he had access to a remarkable library of Greek works belonging to the sultan of Bukhara, and made the fullest use of his time. Before he was eighteen, he reckoned, he had assimilated all the scientific and philosophical knowledge available, so that thereafter he added nothing to his store of information, though his understanding of it deepened. Perhaps it was well that he had read so widely while he had the opportunity, for about 998 his circumstances changed. On his father's death he had to seek a civil service appointment to make a living. The political conditions of the region also altered for the worse; and the rise and fall of small dynasties and administrations meant that he had constantly to move from place to place. From about 1015 to 1022 he was in Hamadhan, and for part of this time occupied the difficult and dangerous post of vizier or chief minister to the local Buwayhid prince. From about 1023 until his death he was in Ispahan, under the patronage of the local prince.

In considering Avicenna as a philosopher, it must also be remembered that his *Canon of Medicine* holds an outstanding place in medical science, and that his writings on other sciences were also influential. His philosophy is contained chiefly in two books the *Shifā'* and the *Najāt*, of which the first is a great compendium including sciences as well as philosophy, while the second is an abridged version of the philosophical parts of the longer work. This second is divided into three parts, one dealing with logic, one with "natural philosophy" (really questions about such matters as substance and accident and the nature of the human soul), and one about "theology' (including cosmology). The general position is Neoplatonic. God is the One, the "necessarily existent" (*wājib al-wujūd*), from whom everything emanates. Beneath him are the pure intelligences and the spheres. The conception of the human soul is essentially Aristotelian, but modified apparently in accordance with the discussions and interpretations of later Greek platonizing philosophers. Like most of the other Islamic philosophers he explains the possibility of prophethood; but where al-Fārābī had connected prophethood with the highest form of imagination, Avicenna links it with the highest part of the soul, the intellect.

It is also worth noting that in contrast to al-Fārābī, there is no trace of Shīʿism in Avicenna, that is, no attempt to show that the actual ruler receives a more than ordinary portion of divine wisdom. He is mainly concerned to explain how through a prophet a state based on divine wisdom may be established in the first place. This change of emphasis and apparent avoidance of Shīʿism is perhaps chiefly due to the fact that by this time Fāṭimid propaganda was active in the east of the Islamic world. Avicenna himself remembered how when he was a boy propagandists had arrived in Bukhara and how he had overheard heated discussions about the teaching they gave. In his maturity even Imāmite-Shīʿite rulers must have realized that this propaganda was a threat to their power; and anything resembling it would therefore be suspect. Another relevant point is that Avicenna had as much political power as he wanted, and does not seem to have felt in any way the rivalry of Sunnite ulema. Thus there was nothing to lead him to exaggerate the importance of philosophy. In this respect he was in a similar position to the Muʿtazilites during the period of their political ascendancy; and like them he took for granted that his philosophical interpretation of Islam was the true one. An identification of their own interpretation with the true Islam was likewise common among mystics; and Avicenna had also a mystic side.

The final questions concerning Avicenna are about the relation of his philosophy to his mysticism and to his religious outlook generally. To begin with the latter, he was brought up as a good Muslim, he memorized the Qur'ān and he studied the Sharīʿa or revealed law. In the autobiographical fragment he tells us that he went to the mosque and prayed about his intellectual problems, and he says nothing about any conscious change in his views. He probably felt that the Greek scientific and philosophical learning belonged to a different sphere from Islamic doctrine, and that there was no fundamental opposition between them. In his philosophy he seems to have thought of himself as supporting and elucidating what he considered to be the central doctrines of Islam—the existence of God who is the source of all being, and the possibility of men becoming prophets and receiving revelations. Avicenna's conception of prophethood and his conception of the soul's journey to God are closely linked both with one another and with his philosophy. Nineteenth-century European scholars thought that his mysticism was extraneous to his philosophy, but fuller acquaintance with his writings makes it clear that this is not so. His mysticism and his philosophy constitute a single integrated system. The extent of his mystical writings shows that the mystical life meant much to him. It was presumably the source of his intellectual energy. Because of this personal religious attitude Avicenna has been held by one of the leading modern scholars to come closer to the spirit of Plato than other philosophers whose style is more Platonic and less Aristotelian. "He understood something which is the very essence of Plato's thought, and it may be that for this reason he appealed to religious Muslims—as Plato himself has conveyed religious truth, to people open to religion, at all times." [5]

BIBLIOGRAPHY

G. M. WICKENS (ed.), *Avicenna: Scientist and Philosopher*, London, 1952; six lectures delivered at Cambridge to mark the millenary, including one by A. J. Arberry on his life. Criticized by S. van den Bergh in *Bulletin of the School of Oriental and African Studies*, xvi (1954), 400-4.

A.-M. GOICHON, *La Philosophie d'Avicenne et son influence en Europe médiévale*, Paris, 1944; three lectures on the purely philosophical aspects of his achievements. Also: *La Distinction de l'essence et de l'existence d'après Ibn Sīnā*, Paris, 1937; philosophical discussion. Also: *Livre des directives et remarques*, Beirut and Paris, 1951; translation of a general exposition of his system.

Louis GARDET, *La Pensée religieuse d'Avicenne*, Paris, 1951; a careful and sympathetic study of his relation to Sunnite theology and of his mysticism.

Henry CORBIN, *Avicenna and the Visionary Recital*, London, 1961; a fascinating exploration of his mystical and theosophical thought; the relation of later Imāmite Shī'ism to him is discussed in pp. 243-57.

F(azlur-) RAHMAN, *Avicenna's Psychology*, London, 1952; translation of section of *K. an-Najāt* with notes. Also: *Prophecy in Islam*, London, 1958; deals with the philosophical conception of prophethood.

Soheil M. AFNAN, *Avicenna, his life and works*, London, 1958; careful description; pp. 233-57 on his influence in the east covers much unfamiliar ground.

CHAPTER 11

THE VICISSITUDES OF SHĪʿISM

IT was seen in an earlier chapter (6) that after the death of the eleventh imām and the disappearance of the twelfth in 874 IMĀMITE Shīʿism began to take a definite form and to become organized. After the establishment of the Shīʿite Buwayhids as rulers in Baghdad in 945 the Imāmites gained a measure of official recognition for their legal rite and a corpus of Imāmite jurisprudence began to develop.[6] Along with this went the formulation of their theological position. A statement of this, entitled *Tract on the Beliefs of the Imāmites*, by ash-Shaykh aṣ-Ṣadūq (d. 991), is now available in English.[7] The Imāmites are not far removed in outlook from some of the Muʿtazilites and speak, for example, of the Qur'ān as created; but the precise form and channel of Muʿtazilite influence is not clear. Later material shows that they made use of the conceptions of philosophical theology and criticized the Ashʿarites.[8] Thus the Imāmites were in some sense in the main stream of Islamic theology. On the other hand, the views criticized are seldom those of contemporary or recent opponents, and this suggests that few Imāmite theologians were engaged in active polemics. Until much further study is done it is hardly possible to say more than this.

The ZAYDITE branch of Shīʿism also remains theologically in obscurity, though something is known about certain minor political successes. There was a small state in various regions to the south of the Caspian Sea from about 870 to 1126. Another state, established before 900 in the Yemen, has managed to survive until the present time in one form or another under the Zaydite imāms of Ṣanʿāʾ. This has meant the development of a special Zaydite form of jurisprudence, but it is very close to the four recognized Sunnite rites, and may almost be reckoned a fifth along with them. The Zaydites are more closely connected with the Muʿtazilites than are the Imāmites, and from some points of view seem to be identical with a section of the Muʿtazilites, though there are also references to the conversion of people from a Zaydite position to a Muʿtazilite one. The answer to these riddles is probably to be found by a better understanding of what it meant to be a Zaydite in Baghdad in the earlier part of the ninth century.[9] The Zaydite states, of course, were in somewhat remote mountainous regions, and, though from time to time they had good scholars, could not be expected to play any part in the general development of Islamic theology.

About the ISMĀʿĪLITE form of Shīʿism there is rather more to be said. It must be kept in mind, however, that, though Ismāʿīlism was associated with the Fāṭimid dynasty in Egypt, as a doctrine it had a certain life independent of the Fāṭimids. The Qarmaṭians in the east of Arabia, for example, sometimes acknowledged the suzerainty of the Fāṭimids and sometimes fought against them. Some of the Sunnite writers tried to explain Ismāʿīlism as a resurgence of the old pre-Islamic religions, and the earlier European scholars tended to see in it a Persian national or racial movement. The latter suggestion is clearly wrong, since many non-Persians were Ismāʿīlites, while the Persian ruling classes mostly became Sunnites. Recent scholarly opinion therefore has come to regard Ismāʿīlism as essentially a series of revolutionary movements among labourers, artisans and other depressed classes. Dissatisfaction with the existing state of affairs probably led to a temper of revolt in many centres. It was in part the Ismā'īlite leaders' genius for organization that enabled them to produce a semblance of unity out of numerous disparate groups scattered over a wide area, and to create a revolutionary underground movement with a not-too-definite doctrinal basis. The chief point was obedience to one's superiors within the movement, together with the belief that the commands from one's superiors ultimately came from the imām himself and were infallible.

The movement is said to have been organized in a number of grades, each of which was given more instruction than the one below it. At the lowest level what was said was adapted to the position of the persons involved and to the religious beliefs they had hitherto held. At a slightly higher stage the members were apparently taught that truth in the positive religions was always relative, and that whatever truth there was in them was taken up into Ismā'īlism. In dealing with Muslims they made use of a distinction between external (*ẓāhir*) and internal (*bāṭin*). They claimed that the Qur'ān, besides its external or obvious meaning, had an internal or hidden meaning, and that this inner meaning could be learnt only from the imām. Because of this point of their teaching they are sometimes called Bāṭinites.

The Ismā'īlites hold that after the imām Ismā'īl—the son of Ja'far aṣ-Ṣādiq from whom they derive their name—there were several hidden imāms, until at length the son of one of these founded the Fāṭimid state in 909. The FĀṬIMIDS, because of their general doctrinal position, claimed to be themselves the rightful caliphs of the Islamic community and did not recognize the 'Abbāsids as suzerains. After their conquest of Egypt, too, they had high hopes of being able to give effect to this claim, and intensified their propaganda in the regions acknowledging the ʽAbbāsids. For a moment, in the confusion just before the Seljūqs established themselves in Baghdad, a Turkish general professing allegiance to the Fāṭimids occupied the city, and for nearly a year they instead of the ʽAbbāsids were mentioned in the Friday prayers. After this, however, the tide receded, and it became increasingly clear that the Fāṭimids were unlikely to progress eastwards from Syria, which they occupied for a time. It has been suggested that after the founding of their state the Fāṭimids began to tone down the revolutionary element in their propaganda, and to emphasize rather their superior claims to the caliphate. Be this as it may, it is certain that before 1100 it had proved impossible for those responsible for orderly government in Egypt to satisfy at the same time the aspirations of Asian revolutionaries.

Among the groups belonging to the Fāṭimid movement in its early stages is probably to be reckoned a coterie of philosophers and natural scientists who lived in Basra towards the end of the tenth century. They called themselves the Brethren of Purity or Sincere Brethren (*Ikhwān aṣ-Ṣafā*), and have left behind a collection of fifty or fifty-one Epistles (*Rasā'il*). Nineteenth-century European scholars were greatly impressed by these Epistles and regarded them as a kind of encyclopaedia of the sciences of the day. It has gradually been realized, however, that their apparent learning is somewhat superficial, until a recent writer characterizes them as "revolution masquerading as scientific enlightenment".[10] They were certainly eclectics with a tendency to mystical Neopythagoreanism; and like most Ismā'īlites they were inclined to regard the positive religions, including even Islam, as possessing only relative truth.

Under the title *A Creed of the Fāṭimids* there has been published a summary of Ismā'īlite doctrine which may be taken to represent what was held under the Fāṭimids, though the author died in 1215, nearly half a century after the fall of the dynasty in 1171.[11] The work is essentially a positive presentation of the doctrinal position, without any explicit argument against those holding other positions; but this form of Islam is shown to be the true Islam, and the author has so worded his assertions that Sunnite and other non-Ismāʿīlite doctrines are clearly denied. There is some familiarity with the conceptions of Sunnite philosophical theology, but there can have been no overt discussion. It was an essential Ismāʿīlite principle that human reason is subject to limitations and cannot reach the fullness of truth, which can only be received from the Prophet or one of the Imāms. On such a basis there can be no philosophical theology. Thus, though there are numerous Ismāʿīlite works now accessible and waiting to be studied, they can at most give more detailed information about the evolution of doctrine. Despite the fact, however, that the Ismāʿīlites did not participate in theological discussions with other Muslims, they were an important influence on the general course of theological development, since for a considerable period Sunnism had to be defended intellectually against them.

Long before the final eclipse of the Fāṭimid dynasty a serious split had occurred within the Ismāʿīlite movement, probably due in the last resort to the incompatibility between the interests of responsible administrators and irresponsible revolutionaries. In the Asian section of the Islamic world there were many of the latter. As the Fāṭimid government became more averse to taking aggressive action in Asia, and more incapable of it, the patience of the revolutionaries became exhausted and an insurrection broke out. This was successful in capturing Alamut and other fortresses in mountainous districts, but completely failed to gain any important city or dislodge the Seljūqs. The point of theological interest is what happened on the death of the Fāṭimid imām al-Mustanṣir in 1094 (after reigning from 1035). The vizier, who was the real ruler of Egypt, managed to have the designated heir, Nizār, replaced by another son al-Musta'lī; and the Persian and Syrian revolutionaries took advantage of this happening to break their connection with Egypt by professing to follow Nizār. The interesting thing is that, though Nizār disappeared, having presumably been murdered, the Asian leaders claimed that he was in hiding and that they were still in touch with him. Indeed in 1164 the new Lord of Alamut claimed to have received two letters from him, and on the basis of these inaugurated a curious phase in the life of this sect, "the era of the Resurrection".[12]

The later history of the Ismā'īlites is mainly political, though some theological works exist. The followers of Nizār came to be noted for their practice of political murder, and have added their name of "Assassins" to most European languages; it is derived from an Arabic word (probably in the form *ḥashshāshīn*) meaning "those who use the drug *ḥashīsh*", but it is not certainly known why they were so called. The Crusaders had many picturesque tales about them and their leader, "the old man of the mountain". They and the followers of al-Musta'lī each divided into two groups, and all the groups, at least in part, eventually found their way to India.

This is an appropriate point at which to mention the existence of certain sects which have become so extreme that it is doubtful whether they can still be said to belong to Islam. The religion of the DRUSES (who live mostly in the mountains of the Lebanon, the Hauran and round Damascus) developed out of Ismā'īlism by accepting the Fāṭimid caliph al-Ḥākim (996–1021) as the final incarnation of deity; but other old Middle-Eastern religious ideas have been incorporated. Another sect whose beliefs are derived largely from Ismāʿīlism are the NUṢAYRĪS or ʿALAWITES (in French, Alaouites), who inhabit various parts of Syria and have small groups scattered in other parts of the Middle East. One of their distinctive beliefs is that they regard ʿAlī as an incarnation of deity superior to Muḥammad. Their name, like other names of sects in the Middle East, is often used loosely, and it is sometimes difficult to be certain that the people thus called are indeed members of the sect. Finally, there are the YEZIDIS or Devil-worshippers, who are nearly all Kurds; though their name is Islamic, it is difficult to know whether their religion grew out of Islam or is a development of something older.[13] All these sects constituted small local communities which were almost entirely cut off from the general intellectual and cultural life of the Islamic world.

BIBLIOGRAPHY

M. G. S. HODGSON, *The Order of Assassins*, 's-Gravenhage, 1955; deals mainly with the external history of the movement, but has some theological material.

Wilferd MADELUNG, "Das Imamat in der frühen ismailitischen Lehre", *Der Islam*, xxxvii (1961), 43-135; studies thoroughly hitherto unused sources of information.

F. DIETERICI, *Die Philosophie der Araber im X. Jahrhundert*, Leipzig, 1876, 1879; translations of part of the epistles of the Ikhwān aṣ-Ṣafāʾ.

Adel AWA, *L'Esprit critique des "frères de la Pureté"*, Beirut, 1948; a Paris doctoral thesis.

CHAPTER 12

THE PROGRESS OF SUNNITE THEOLOGY

AFTER 950 many of the actual works of the theologians are extant, but in some respects this makes the study more difficult. Most of the books are still only in manuscript, and some of those that are printed are long. It is often far from obvious, too, how the detailed arguments of a bygone age are relevant to any questions of importance even to their authors, far less to us. Thus the study of Islamic theology in this period can be wearisome, and on the whole has attracted far less attention than that of the early formative period.

Although it is possible to give an account of al-Ashʿarī himself, the origins of the Ashʿarite school are obscure. It has even been suggested that he was only one of many who were introducing rational methods into theology and that it was largely chance that caused him later to be adopted as figure-head. This certainly goes too far. He had, of course, had predecessors from Ḍirār to al-Muḥāsibī who had opposed Muʿtazilite doctrine while accepting Muʿtazilite methods; but al-Ashʿarī's books give every reason for accepting the view that it was he who first used Muʿtazilite methods in such a way that they were acceptable to the main body of Sunnite opinion. His were the only books of this kind, apparently, that later generations could profitably study; and there is thus no reason for thinking that some other unnamed men of the period were just as influential. Yet it must be admitted that we know hardly anything about his immediate followers apart from a few names, and that there cannot have been any important Ash'arite school in the generation immediately following him. What probably happened is that theology had a minor place in a school devoted mainly to the study of Tradition or jurisprudence.

The first theologian about whom it is possible to say much is AL-BĀQILLĀNĪ (the qāḍī Abū-Bakr Muḥammad ibn-Ṭayyib). Even of him biographical details are scanty. He was born in Basra and seems to have spent most of his life in Baghdad. He is said to have visited Shiraz, and also to have been sent on an embassy to the Byzantine court by the Buwayhid sultan. He was trained as a Mālikite jurist, but also studied theology under at least two pupils of al-Ash'arī. He died in 1013.

According to Ibn-Khaldūn (d. 1406) he introduced atomism into Ash'arite theology, but the most recent studies make it clear that this is mistaken, since atomistic conceptions are found in some of al-Ash'arī's own works and were also present in those of his Mu'tazilite predecessors. Two books by al-Bāqillānī, however, give an indication of the new problems that were engaging the attention of the theologians at this period. One was on the *i'jāz* or miraculous character of the Qur'ān, while the other was on the difference between the apologetic miracle (the miracle demonstrating the truth of a prophet's claims) and similar phenomena, whether these be miraculous happenings connected with holy men but not substantiating any claims, or trickery, magic and sorcery.[14] These two subjects are closely linked with one another.

It was inevitable that this problem would sooner or later have to be faced by Islamic theologians using a rational method. Even during the lifetime of Muḥammad the Muslims had in effect been asked: How can you be sure that Muḥammad really is a prophet with a message from God? The Jews of Medina had expressed it more forcibly—"Muḥammad claims to be a prophet in the Biblical tradition, but some of his alleged revelations contradict the Bible, and so he cannot be a prophet". After the Muslim conquest of Iraq, Syria and Egypt, the Muslims were constantly rubbing shoulders with Christians also, and having to learn to live with people who denied Muḥammad's prophethood. Popular theology took the simple line of discovering miracles for Muḥammad or inventing them, but the more serious theologians preferred to base their belief on the miraculous character of the Qur'ān. Again on the popular side, verses which probably meant something else were interpreted to mean that Muḥammad could not read, so as to enhance the miracle of his production of this book.

A fresh element entered in when the mystic al-Ḥallāj (d. 922) claimed that certain miraculous happenings showed that his spiritual experiences were genuine. This provoked discussion over a large field, and many alleged that the happenings were due to trickery or sorcery. With al-Bāqillānī theology adopts the position that the apologetic miracle must be something which only God can do, and which he in fact causes to happen after a prophet has foretold that God will do this to substantiate his prophethood. The claim and prediction were things which ruled out mere conjuring. To rule out trickery by one who made false spiritual claims al-Bāqillānī insisted that the happening should be a violation of the normal course of events which only God had power to bring about. It was always necessary, of course, to use one's wits to notice trickery.

The conclusion that was reached by al-Bāqillānī and many Sunnites was that the Qur'ān itself was the miracle that showed that Muḥammad was a prophet. Its miraculousness lay in its eloquence or sublime literary qualities. Muḥammad is told in the Qur'ān (11.16/13) to challenge the most eloquent of the Arabs to produce the like of it, but none was able to take up the challenge. At times it seems to be hinted that this failure to meet the challenge is due to God's preventing them from doing so; this, being something that only God can do, is further evidence for the miraculousness of the Qur'ān. It is, even from the European point of view, a strong argument, though the European might want to express the conclusions to be drawn from it in more psychological terms. Towards the end of Muḥammad's life and immediately after his death several men and a woman appeared in various parts of Arabia and claimed to be prophets; here, as was usual in the Middle East, religion was bound closely to politics, namely, resistance to the new and growing Islamic state. A few verses by one of the men, in a style reminiscent of the Qur'ān, have been preserved; but these only underline the undeniable fact that nothing comparable to the Qur'ān was produced in Arabia by Muḥammad's contemporaries, or indeed by later generations.

In the present state of our studies it is difficult to assess precisely the place of al-Bāqillānī in the development of Ash'arism. Little has been preserved of the works by Ash'arites of the period who were apparently of comparable standing, such as Ibn-Fūrak (d. 1015), who seems to have been latterly an opponent of the Karrāmites in Ghazna, and Abū-Is'ḥāq al-Isfarā'inī (d. 1027), who taught theology in a school or college built for him in Nishapur. Al-Bāqillānī probably had little to say that was original, except in the case of the apologetic miracle, but he brought material together and set out in orderly fashion the whole range of Ash'arite teaching, and he was also active in the dissemination of it.

From this time on the names of many distinguished scholars are known who were Ash'arites in theology. Only two will be mentioned here, and both of these spent most of their lives in Nishapur. The first is often known simply as AL-BAGHDĀDĪ, but his full name is Abū-Manṣūr ʿAbd-al-Qāhir ibn-Ṭāhir; he died in 1037. He is best known for an account of the early sects, which points out clearly the errors of each; but he also wrote a compendium of Ashʿarite theological doctrine, which gives a lucid exposition of the main points and notes the main differences from the sects. The second is AL-QUSHAYRĪ (d. 1072) who is one of the great writers on Islamic mysticism. His presence among the Ashʿarites—and he wrote, and presumably lectured, on theology—is a reminder that the cleavage between theology and mysticism must not be exaggerated, since it was never absolute.

With the Seljūq entry into Baghdad in 1055 and their acceptance of the nominal suzerainty of the caliph, it might have been thought, since they were Sunnites, that life would become easier for the Ashʿarites. Instead they had for a time to meet persecution. The reasons for this are not clear, but it was the work of the Seljūq sultan's vizier, al-Kundurī, who was apparently instructed to take measures against heretics, that is, primarily the Shīʿites, but who also included the Ashʿarites; it is said to have been due to the fact that he was a Ḥanafite and bitterly opposed to the Shāfiʿites. For a time the Ashʿarites were publicly cursed in the mosques at the Friday midday service, and forbidden to teach or preach. Several, including al-Qushayrī and al-Juwaynī, decided it was safer to flee or go into hiding. Al-Juwaynī spent about four years in the Ḥijāz and from this came to be known as Imām al-Ḥaramayn, the imām of the two sanctuaries, Mecca and Medina. This must have been from about 1059 to 1063.

The death of one Seljūq sultan and the accession to the throne of another, Alp-Arslān, led to a complete reversal of fortune for the Ashʿarites. The new sultan had a powerful and capable vizier, NIẒĀM-AL-MULK, who was a personal rival of al-Kundurī and also had already been associated with Shāfiʿites and Ashʿarites. He was aware of the danger from Fāṭimid propaganda and realized that it could not be averted merely by repressive measures. He therefore conceived a far-reaching policy for the intellectual (theological) defence of the Sunnite hegemony, and in this the central post was given to the Ashʿarites. The cursing of them on Fridays was stopped, and towards the end of 1065 the building of a new college in Baghdad, the Niẓāmiyya, was begun. After the opening of this college in 1067 the Ḥanbalites of Baghdad, who resented its predominantly Ashʿarite character, caused some trouble which led to rioting. Niẓām-al-Mulk, without withdrawing his support from the Ashʿarites, made some concessions which reduced the tensions. He also proceeded to create a series of similar colleges in other important cities of the caliphate. An influential one was the Niẓāmiyya at Nishapur where al-Juwaynī was professor and al-Ghazālī a student.

AL-JUWAYNĪ, the Imām of the Two Sanctuaries, came from a scholarly family. His father had opened some sort of a school for jurisprudence and related subjects at Nishapur about 1016, and on the father's death in 1046 al-Juwaynī the younger (also called Abū-'l-Maʿālī), though only twenty or less, took over the conduct of the school, while himself continuing to study certain subjects. Pressure from the Seljūq government, which controlled Nishapur for several years before it gained the supreme power in Baghdad, caused him to abandon Nishapur and betake himself to Baghdad. This was possibly about 1054, and was doubtless the operation against heretics already mentioned. Eventually, after Baghdad too was firmly in Seljūq hands, he retired to Mecca and Medina. About 1063 he was able to return to Nishapur. This was one of the cities where Niẓām-al-Mulk established a Niẓāmiyya college, and al-Juwaynī was head of it until his death in 1085.

Al-Juwaynī's theological position can conveniently be studied in a French translation of a comprehensive work called the *Irshād* or *Right Guidance.*[15] In general his position is very similar to that of al-Bāqillānī, but the arguments are more elaborate and more refined. On the whole the points of interest are the same, but there is a more definite concern for epistemological preliminaries. Apart from this the chief matter to notice is an apparent slight shift from the position of al-Ash'arī himself towards that of the Mu'tazilites. One sign of this is the acceptance of the doctrine of the "states" (*aḥwāl*) associated with the Mu'tazilite Abū-Hāshim. More important is the admission of "metaphorical interpretation" (*ta'wīl*) of anthropomorphic terms applied to God, where it can be shown that the literal sense is impossible. Thus, whereas al-Ash'arī had held that "hand" as applied to God was to be understood "without explaining precisely how", al-Juwaynī argued that the corporeal meaning was impossible and that it must be understood as "power". The biographers also state that al-Juwaynī studied philosophy, and, though there is no trace of this in his writings, it seems likely that it was he who brought his great pupil al-Ghazālī to realize the importance of studying philosophy. At the end of his life, however, after his quest for truth even in books of which the strict theologians disapproved, he came back to something like a child-like faith, and summed up the results of his whole experience of life in the advice, "Hold to the religion of the old women".

Bibliography

J. Bouman, *Le Conflit autour du Coran et la solution d'al-Bāqillānī*, Amsterdam, 1959; careful discussion.

W. Montgomery Watt, "Some Muslim Discussions of Anthropomorphism", *Transactions of the Glasgow University Oriental Society*, xiv (1953), 1-10.

R. Paret, "Der Standpunkt Al-Bāqillānī's in der Lehre vom Koran", *Studi orientalistici in onore di G. Levi della Vida*, Rome, 1956, ii. 294 ff.

Imam el Haramein (Jowayni), *El-Irchad*, ed. and tr. into French by J. D. Luciani, Paris, 1938 (with some corrections by G. Vajda in *Journal Asiatique*, 1938, 149-53).

A. J. Arberry, *The Doctrine of the Ṣūfīs*, Cambridge, 1935; translation of *K. at-Taʿarruf* by al-Kalābādhī (d. 995); pp. 14-74 deal with dogmatic questions on Ḥanafite lines.

CHAPTER 13

AL-GHAZĀLĪ

Al-Ghazālī has been acclaimed by both Muslim and European scholars as the greatest Muslim after Muḥammad. Whether this judgement is in fact sound is a particularly difficult question for European scholars to settle, since for most of them al-Ghazālī is undoubtedly the most congenial and most approachable of Muslim theological writers. Perhaps the safest thing to say would be that the question cannot be properly answered until there has been a careful study of all the religious phenomena of the period of two hundred years after his death to see how far his influence can be traced.[16]

He is commonly known as al-Ghazālī or Algazel, but there has been a dispute almost from his own time whether the word should be spelt "Ghazālī" or "Ghazzālī". There can be no certainty, but the former is on the whole preferable. Those who adopt the latter usually take it to imply that his father was a poor spinner and vendor of wool (*ghazzāl*), but this can hardly be correct since the great theologian had an uncle or granduncle also called al-Ghazālī who was distinguished as a scholar. He is often referred to by Arabic writers by his "father-name" (*kunya*) of Abū-Ḥāmid ("father of Ḥāmid"). His own name was Muḥammad, and he had a brother called Aḥmad, who was noted as a mystic and wrote books in Persian. The theologian was born at Ṭus (near the modern Meshhed in Persia) in 1058, and received his early education there. For the later stages of his education he went afield, as was the custom, first to Gurgan

(Jurjān) at the south-east corner of the Caspian Sea, and then, perhaps about 1077, to the nearer Nishapur. Here besides continuing his legal studies he was introduced to theology and possibly also philosophy by al-Juwaynī. On the death of al-Juwaynī in 1085 he went to the "camp" of Niẓām-al-Mulk, and took a prominent place among the many scholars there, so that in 1091, while still very young, he was appointed to a professorship at the Niẓāmiyya college in Baghdad.

For four years he was a popular lecturer here with over three hundred students in his audience. At the same time he was by private reading gaining a thorough grasp of the philosophy of al-Fārābī and Avicenna—something no theologian had hitherto done. First he wrote a lengthy objective summary of their views (which was translated into Latin in the Middle Ages and because of its lucidity became influential). Then he wrote a devastating criticism of their views, *The Inconsistency of the Philosophers*. He also produced several other works about the same time. Despite his phenomenal outward success, however, he was sick at heart, and felt he was in grave danger of hell-fire. In July 1095 the inner conflicts produced a physical symptom, an impediment in speech which prevented him from lecturing. After several months of great interior suffering he left Baghdad in November 1095, ostensibly to make the Pilgrimage to Mecca, but really with the firm intention of abandoning his career as a jurist, theologian and university professor in order to serve God more completely as a poor sufi (mystic). The reality of this conversion has been questioned and various material motives have been suggested for his great change. None seems sufficient to account entirely for it; but it is possible that bad relations with the new Seljūq ruler Barkiyāruq, who was recognized in Baghdad in February 1095, was a factor in his decision. A deeper reason was his disgust at the blatant worldliness of most of his colleagues among the ulema (the jurists and other scholars); and it may be that his chief reason for abandoning his career was the impossibility, as he felt, of living an upright life in this environment. This would be a natural reaction for a man of real piety coming to the sophistication of the capital from the comparatively simple life of a provincial centre.

From Baghdad he went first to Damascus. A misinterpretation of one of his own statements has led many scholars, both ancient and modern, to think that he spent the next ten years between Syria and the Ḥijaz; but more careful study of all the available source-material makes it clear that this was not so, and that the ten years of withdrawal from the world were spent rather as follows.[17] He did not go on pilgrimage immediately after his departure from Baghdad, but waited until the pilgrimage of the following year, in November and December 1096. Either before or in the course of his journey to Mecca he visited Jerusalem and Hebron, but he almost certainly did not go to Egypt, as is sometimes stated. Soon after the pilgrimage he returned to Iraq, for he was seen in Baghdad in June, 1097. After a stay there lasting a few months or perhaps more than a year he returned to his native town of Ṭus, where he lived the life of an ascetic and mystic and gathered round him a community of disciples; these shared his practices and received instruction from him.

At the end of 1104 there was another change of Seljūq ruler, and the post of vizier came into the hands of a son of Niẓām-al-Mulk who prevailed on al-Ghazālī to return to academic lecturing in Nishapur, presumably in the Niẓāmiyya college. One of the considerations that weighed with him was a Tradition in which Muḥammad asserted that at the beginning of each century a "renewer" of his religion would appear; they were now in the closing months of the fifth Islamic century, and many friends assured him that he was the destined "renewer" for the next century. So to Nishapur he went in July 1106 (xi. 499 A.H.), and remained there at least three years. Finally, whether because of ill-health or for some other reason we do not know, he returned to Ṭus, and died there in December 1111.

The fullness of our knowledge of al-Ghazālī's life is largely due to the fact that he has left us an autobiographical work, whose title may be translated *Deliverance from Error*. It is primarily an intellectual apologia, and for this reason his life has been treated in it schematically rather than chronologically. He recounts how, after a period of sheer scepticism, he set out on a quest for truth, and examined in turn the results achieved by the four main classes of "seekers after truth" in his own day, the theologians, the philosophers, the Ismā'īlites and the sufis. It is this framework which is suspect chronologically; yet it is convenient to follow it (with one change of order) in considering his contributions to the thought of his time.

Al-Ghazālī's study of philosophy deeply affected all he afterwards did, and indeed the whole subsequent course of Islamic theology. As al-Ash'arī by combining Mu'tazilite and Ḥanbalite views overcame the first wave of Greek influence, so by bringing together philosophy and theology al-Ghazālī overcame the second wave, that is, the philosophical movement culminating in Avicenna. His attitude was far from purely negative, however. On the one hand, indeed, he argued powerfully against Neoplatonism in *The Inconsistency of the Philosophers*, and after this there was no further philosopher of note in the eastern Islamic world (though, since Avicenna died in 1037, philosophy was probably already in decline from other causes before al-Ghazālī wrote in 1095).[18] On the other hand, he was carried away by admiration for Aristotelian syllogistic logic, wrote several books about it and thus introduced it to other theologians and jurists for whom the books of the philosophers were inaccessible or technically difficult. In brief, where al-Ashʿarī had defended the central Sunnite dogmas by Muʿtazilite methods, al-Ghazālī defended them by the far superior Neoplatonic (including Aristotelian) methods and concepts which he had learnt from Avicenna and others. It was because of this change that Ibn-Khaldūn spoke of al-Ghazālī as being the first theologian to write according to "the way of the moderns".

To theology al-Ghazālī's contribution is not important, apart from his introduction of philosophical methods. He produced one work, *The Golden Mean in Belief*, which, though shorter, is similar to the *Right Guidance* of al-Juwaynī. There is an introduction dealing with the nature and importance of syllogism, and some of the arguments are given syllogistic form; but otherwise the slight differences between this and al-Juwaynī's work are comparable to those between al-Juwaynī and al-Bāqillānī.

Al-Ghazālī might have made greater contributions to theology in matters of detail had he not to some extent turned away from it at his conversion to sufism. The words "to some extent" here must be emphasized, for it has sometimes been supposed that he entirely abandoned theology. What happened rather was that he became aware of the limitations of theology, and realized that it was not by theological learning but by the sufistic life of moral uprightness and closeness to God that man attained to heaven. Theology still remained, however, as a necessary safeguard for true belief. *The Golden Mean* was possibly not completed till after his conversion. His great work *The Revival of the Religious Sciences* contains a creed for memorizing and a short exposition of general Sunnite doctrine. In a later summary of the

Revival known as *The Forty* he speaks of *The Golden Mean* with qualified approval, as better than most books of its kind. Finally, since about 1959 it has been known to scholars that about a fortnight before he died he finished an essay entitled *The Restraining of the Commonalty from the Science of Theology*; and in this essay his theological position is still Ash'arite. Thus he never really ceased to be an Ash'arite theologian, though he came to think theology in general less important than he had once done.

His study of Ismā'īlism was probably rather different from that of philosophy and theology, and it is doubtful whether he expected to learn much from it. In view of the political threat from Fāṭimid propaganda, however, he was requested by the 'Abbāsid caliph (whose position was more threatened than that of the Seljūq sultans) to write a critique of the intellectual or theological aspects of this propaganda. This he must have done between February 1094 and his departure from Baghdad in 1095. He also wrote one or two smaller books on particular points. How influential these were is difficult to say, but they doubtless contributed to the defeat of Ismā'īlism. The revolt which began in 1090 with successes in mountainous districts did not gain any town, while in 1094 the insurgents broke with the Fāṭimid government. (Al-Ghazālī usually refers to the Ismā'īlites by other names such as Ta'līmites and Bāṭinites.)

Though in his own account of his development al-Ghazālī speaks as if he began to study sufism only after completing his studies of philosophy and Ismā'īlism, he had been in contact with sufis from an early age. On his father's death he and his brother had been under the guardianship of a friend who was a sufi; and during his student days at Nishapur he was influenced by a professor (probably of jurisprudence), al-Fārmadhī (d. 1084), who was a leader of the sufis there. At that period he seems to have made some acquaintance with sufism both in theory and practice but then to have turned from it to theology and philosophy. In the spiritual crisis of 1095 he turned again to sufism, but quickly realized that an intellectual understanding of it was not enough, and that he must begin to put it into practice in his life. It was with this thought in mind that he abandoned his post in Baghdad and divested himself of his wealth. Some idea of the outward manner of his life may be gained from a short work *The Beginning of Guidance*. It was really a kind of monastic rule, and the band of disciples he gathered round him at Ṭus had the makings of a monastic community. The conception of the good life on which he based his practice is described in full in *The Revival of the Religious Sciences*. This is a lengthy work in forty "books", which occupies four large volumes in Arabic. A number of single books have been translated into European languages.

Since al-Ghazālī's maturity was thus devoted to the practice of sufism, it is important to try to assess the contribution of this aspect of his achievement to the development of Islamic thought. It must not be supposed that prior to al-Ghazālī there was a complete rift between the sufis and the ulema. Some sufis were heretical, but by no means all. Al-Qushayrī, besides being a leading sufi, was himself one of the ulema. There were even sufis among the Ḥanbalites. Some of the ulema were prepared to accept as orthodox the mystic al-Ḥallāj, who had been executed for heresy in 922. This shows that much of the sufistic movement was close to the main body of Sunnism. One thing that al-Ghazālī did, however, was to bring about a greater degree of fusion. For most of his predecessors, it would seem, sufism began where the canonical practices laid down in the Sharīʿa left off. A large part of al-Ghazālī's work, however, consisted in showing the inner—one might almost say "sufistic"—meaning of the canonical duties binding on every Muslim. The beginning of the truly sufistic life was the faithful observance of all these duties. Only on this foundation could one proceed to the higher mystical "states" which were the special province of sufism. Of these "states" al-Ghazālī was able to write from a measure of personal experience; and this made it clear to all that the "states" did not entail heresy, but could be combined with the faithful observance of the Sharī'a.

In these respects, then, al-Ghazāli was not making a direct contribution to theology; but he was showing that canonical duties and theological formulations of doctrine stood in no merely external relation to a man but could be linked up with his deepest life. This almost certainly contributed to a genuine revival of religion, without which theology might have faded away. Al-Ghazālī also engaged in speculation about the nature of the mystical experiences and their relation to the prophet's experience of revelation—in *The Niche for Lights*, for example; but his speculations were not followed up by later theologians, and do not seem to have been influential in any way.

The account of al-Ghazālī which has been given so far in this survey has assumed the correctness of one view with regard to a series of controversial questions. Recent studies, however, notably the publication of the date of *The Restraining of the Commonalty*, suggest that the opinion of scholars is moving towards the acceptance of this view. The focus of the difficulties is that many works are ascribed to al-Ghazālī whose authenticity has been questioned. One or two were held to be spurious in the century after al-Ghazālī, and doubts have been expressed about the authenticity of several more by Ignaz Goldziher, Duncan Black Macdonald, Miguel Asin Palacios, the present writer and others.

Many of these dubious works engage in mystical

speculations that are quite opposed to Sunnite theology; in one or two there is an acceptance of Neoplatonic doctrines that al-Ghazālī had decisively rejected in his *Inconsistency of the Philosophers*. Those who hold the authenticity of these works therefore postulate a thoroughgoing mystical period in al-Ghazālī's closing years, when he gave himself up completely to extreme forms of mysticism and abandoned both canonical duties and Sunnite dogma. With the discovery, however, of the date of *The Restraining of the Commonalty*, where he is still Sunnite in general theological outlook—unless this date can somehow be shown to be false—the hypothesis of a late extreme mystical period has become untenable. Since it is difficult to find another point in his life at which the dubious works could have been written, there is a strong case for accepting their spurious character. There are a number of cases in the Islamic world of works being falsely ascribed to a man, either to discredit the man or, more often, to gain currency for heretical doctrines by ascribing them to a man of unimpeachable authority.

Bibliography

Margaret Smith, *Al-Ghazālī the Mystic*, London, 1944; has materials about his life not found elsewhere in English.

A. J. Wensinck, *La Pensée de Ghazzālī*, Paris, 1940; essentially a collection of material. This work and the previous one suffer from making use of works of dubious authenticity.

W. Montgomery Watt, *Muslim Intellectual: the Struggle and Achievement of al-Ghazali*, Edinburgh, 1963; attempts to set his life and thought in the context of his age.

Maurice BOUYGES, *Essai de chronologie des œuvres de al-Ghazali*, ed. and brought up to date by M. Allard, Beirut, 1959; contains a mass of valuable bibliographical information, and also discusses questions of authenticity. The latter are discussed in Montgomery Watt's articles, "A Forgery in al-Ghazālī's *Mishkāt?*", "The Authenticity of the Works Attributed to al-Ghazālī", *Journal of the Royal Asiatic Society*, 1949, 5-22; 1952, 24-45.

J. OBERMANN, *Der philosophische und religiöse Subjektivismus Ghazālis*, Vienna, 1921; useful studies mainly based on the *Revival* (*Iḥya'*), but the conclusions are unduly influenced by philosophical presuppositions.

F. JABRE, *La Notion de certitude selon Ghazali*, Paris, 1958; *La Notion de la Ma'rifa chez Ghazali*, Beirut, 1958; again useful studies based on authentic works but partly vitiated by dubious or erroneous preconceptions.

G. H. BOUSQUET, etc. *Ih'ya 'Ouloûm ed-Dîn ou Vivification des sciences de la foi*, Paris, 1955; French analysis of *The Revival of the Religious Sciences*. Several of the forty books have now been translated into European languages.

W. MONTGOMERY WATT, *The Faith and Practice of al-Ghazāli*, London, 1951; translations of *Deliverance from Error* and *The Beginning of Guidance*.

S. A. KAMALI, *Al-Ghazali's Tahafut al-Falasifah* (*Incoherence of the Philosophers*), Lahore, 1958; a satisfactory translation; much of it is also translated by S. van den Bergh in the refutation of it by Averroes (see Bibliography to ch. 15).

M. ASIN PALACIOS, *El justo medio en la creencia*, Madrid, 1929; Spanish translation of *The Golden Mean in Belief*.

I. GOLDZIHER, *Streitschrift des Gazālī gegen die*

Bāṭinijja-Sekte, Leiden, 1916; introduction, summary and abbreviated edition of a work against the Ismāʿīlites.

W. H. T. GAIRDNER, *Al-Ghazzālī's Mishkāt al-Anwār* ("*The Niche for Lights*"), London, 1924; translation with introduction.

CHAPTER 14

SUNNITE THEOLOGY FROM 1100 TO 1250

In passing from al-Ghazālī to the immediately following period there is a sense of passing from bright sunshine to murky obscurity. Apart from studies of Ibn-Taymiyya (d. 1328) and Muḥammad ʿAbduh (d. 1905) no detailed work has been done on any subsequent thinker in the area of the ʿAbbāsid caliphate. The names of thousands of extant works are to be found in "Brockelmann", but only a handful have been studied even cursorily by Western scholars, and not so very many even by living Muslims. What follows is therefore like an early nineteenth-century map of Africa.

It is relevant to notice here, though it does not strictly belong to the history of theology, a new religious development of the twelfth century or early thirteenth century. This was the beginning of what are usually called dervish orders or dervish fraternities. It was not a complete novelty. There are traces of men living a common life according to a rule soon after 800; and al-Fārmadhī (d. 1084), who influenced al-Ghazālī, seems to have been head of a body of sufis who were beginning to have some of the characteristics of an order. Al-Ghazālī himself, too, as noticed above, instituted something like a monastery-school. By the thirteenth century there had come out of the body once headed by al-Fārmadhī and later by Aḥmad al-Ghazālī three orders with a more definite form and greater permanence than any previous groups of sufis. Other orders soon followed, until orders became an important feature of

Islamic religious life. In many lands at the close of the nineteenth century large numbers of the common people were attached to orders, though as associates rather than full members; and the worship of the order, known as a *dhikr*, seems to have meant more to them than the formal prayers of the Sharīʿa. Since 1900 the influence of the orders has declined in some countries, partly because of their corruption and partly for other reasons. A picture of an order in its decadence will be found in *An Egyptian Childhood* by Taha Husayn.

For the historian of religion these phenomena raise many important questions. Did al-Ghazālī make any direct contribution to this new development, or was he merely one strand in a broad warp of tendencies in the same direction? What was the original attitude of the orders to the formal prayers, and when did people become less interested in these than in the *dhikr*? Was there any underlying reason for such changes? This last question is also relevant to theology, for, as will be seen, great changes came over theology, and it is important to consider whether these changes were connected with those just noted, and, if so, what the connecting links were. So far as the history of theology goes it may be remarked that, though the earlier orders kept to the main Sunnite tradition, some of the later ones held heretical doctrines. These were not worked out in any elaborate theology, however, and the orders do not seem to have entered into serious debate with the theologians or in any way tried to supplant them and take their place in the centre of the intellectual stage.

On turning to Ashʿarite theology the results of al-Ghazālī's studies in philosophy are quickly evident. There are only two important names during a century and a half, but both are of men who have plunged into philosophy with eagerness. The first is ASH-SHAHRASTĀNĪ who receives his name from the small town in eastern Persia where he was born (in 1076 or 1086). He was educated at Nishapur and other places in the region. In 1116 he made the pilgrimage to Mecca, and took the opportunity of his journey to spend three years lecturing or preaching in the Niẓāmiyya college in Baghdad. The rest of his life, however, until his death in 1153, was spent in his homeland. He was accused both of Ismāʿīlite sympathies and activities, and also of supporting the philosophers. His great interest in philosophy is obvious from his works. The charge of Ismāʿīlism is perhaps due to the fact that all his books were written for a patron, the *naqīb al-ashrāf* or dean of the ʿAlids (descendants of ʿAlī) in Tirmidh[19].

Ash-Shahrastānī has already been mentioned as the most important of the heresiographers, but he is also a philosophical theologian in his own right. Two works are accessible: a comprehensive work, called by Alfred Guillaume who edited it and made an abridged translation into English, his *Summa Philosophiae*, and a shorter work criticizing Avicenna on various points. The former is clear evidence of the extent to which philosophy has invaded theology. The order of topics in the work is roughly the same as in similar works of al-Juwaynī and al-Ghazālī, but the method of treatment is transformed. Among the older Islamic theologians whose views have to be criticized and refuted are inserted either the philosophers generally or Avicenna by name. The arguments, too, employ new philosophical conceptions and logical methods, even when the philosophers are not specifically mentioned. Indeed, the views of the older writers are reformulated in terms of the new conceptions, so that the authors, had they been present, might have had difficulty in recognizing their own intellectual progeny.

The other man was FAKHR-AD-DĪN AR-RĀZĪ (1149–1209), the son of a jurist and preacher in Rayy (beside modern Teheran). He was educated as a Shāfiʿite jurist and Ash'arite theologian, but had also a wide knowledge of philosophy and the Greek sciences. At an early period in his career he went to Khwarizm, the region of Central Asia immediately south of the Aral Sea, in order to controvert the Mu'tazilite theology which was apparently still dominant in this little pocket; but he had to retire to Bukhara and Samarqand. Later he is found at Ghazna and in the Punjab; and he finally settled at Herat (in modern Afghanistan), where a *madrasa* or college was built for him. In this final period of his life he was under the patronage of the Ghōrid sultan and the rising dynasty of the Khwarizm-shahs, but despite this he is said to have met his death through poisoning by Karrāmite enemies.

When one looks at his comprehensive theological work, the *Muḥaṣṣal*, one is struck by the growing importance of philosophy as a basis for theology. The book is divided into four roughly equal parts, and of these the first deals with logical and epistemological preliminaries, and the second with the nature of the objects of knowledge (the existent, the necessary, the possible, etc.). Only about the middle of the book does he come on to the doctrine of God in the third part, while the fourth part is devoted to prophethood, eschatology and similar matters. This is an indication of the balance of his interests. Yet it does not mean that he has become altogether a philosopher. His arguments against the Mu'tazilites must not be forgotten. Besides those in Khwarizm he produced a mammoth commentary on the Qur'ān which, though on the one hand introducing philosophical conception in the exegesis of the text, on the other is concerned to refute the Mu'tazilite interpretations of many verses as these are found in the commentary of az-Zamakhsharī (d. 1144). Indeed, despite his philosophizing, ar-Rāzī is more conservative and orthodox than al-Ghazālī in matters of dogma and less ready to speculate freely. For example, there was a Tradition, much discussed by the theologians, in which Muḥammad said that God created Adam in his image (or form); some theologians resorted to ingenious devices to avoid making the pronoun "his" refer to God; the Ḥanbalites mostly accepted it "without stating how"; al-Ghazālī comes near accepting and explaining it; but ar-Rāzī, in showing how "his" can be taken as referring to God turns the whole into an assertion that is entirely about Adam and that says nothing about God.[20] This combination of philosophy and conservatism is symptomatic.

During this period theological activity seems to have continued among the Ḥanafites and Māturīdites, but it has not been studied, apart from an isolated creed. This is the *Articles of Belief* of NAJM-AD-DĪN 'UMAR AN-NASAFĪ (1068–1142),[21] which later became famous and has been frequently commented on down to the present time. The author spent most of his life in and around Samarqand, though he also made the pilgrimage to Mecca, and seems to have been respected as a jurist and Traditionist and not at all as a theologian. About the same time lived another scholar in Farghāna (on the Jaxartes), known as AL-USHĪ (d. 1173), who is chiefly remembered because he composed a creed in the form of a poem of sixty-six lines, and this creed also was much commented on. Thus we do not know anything of any theologizing comparable to that of the Ash'arites, but only of this writing of creeds which points forward to the next phase of theological development.

Of the other theological schools likewise not much is known. The Ḥanbalites were strong and active in Baghdad, but al-Ghazālī speaks of them as relatively weak in his day, and so the presumption is that there were not many Ḥanbalites elsewhere. A certain amount of material about them is now readily accessible, and some of their internal disputes have been studied in detail. One of their bright young men, IBN-ʿAQĪL (d. 1119), was for a time attracted by the Muʿtazilite position, and incurred the displeasure of some of his colleagues.[22] Another interesting fact about the Ḥanbalites is that one of them, ʿABD-AL-QĀDIR AL-JĪLĀNĪ or al-Jīlī (d. 1167), was interested in sufism and came to be accepted as the eponymous founder of one of the early orders, the Qādiriyya.

The KARRĀMITES and the Muʿtazilites have been mentioned in connection with Fakhr-ad-Dīn ar-Rāzī. The latter is also said to have converted large numbers of Karrāmites in Afghanistan; perhaps there was some important change in the local situation as a result of the fall of the Ghaznavid dynasty. The MUʿTAZILITES of this period are also mysterious. For reasons that are not clear they were prominent in Khwarizm (which had also been the home of the Muʿtazilite Qur'ān-commentator az-Zamakhsharī), and al-Jīlānī is said to have visited a Muʿtazilite in Baghdad. Despite the *odium theologicum* they were probably now regarded as holding a somewhat eccentric version of the main Sunnite position, their difference from the Ashʿarites being little more than that of the Māturīdites. This would serve to explain how the commentary of az-Zamakhsharī soon found wide acceptance among scholars of all shades of opinion; its philological merits were taken to outweigh any danger from its heretical views.

BIBLIOGRAPHY

A. GUILLAUME, *The Summa Philosophiae of al-Shahrastāni, Kitāb Nihāyatu 'l-Iqdām*, ed. and tr. London, 1934.

Paul KRAUS, "The Controversies of Fakhr al-dīn

Rāzī', *Islamic Culture*, xii (1938), 131-53 (also in French in *Bulletin de l'Institut d'Egypte*, xix (1937), 187-214).

I. Goldziher, "Aus der Theologie des Fachr al-Din Râzî'", *Der Islam*, iii (1912), 213-47; deals with his treatment of Traditions and emphasis on the sinlessness of prophets; gives details about Mu'tazilites of Khwarizm.

CHAPTER 15

THEOLOGY AND PHILOSOPHY IN THE ISLAMIC WEST

THE Islamic West is a convenient term, parallel to the Arabic *Maghrib*, to designate Islamic Spain and North Africa. This whole region tended to constitute a single unit, with Spain as the senior partner. From the time of its conquest about the beginning of the eighth century the region was under the Umayyad caliphate of Damascus. On the fall of the Umayyads in 750, and before the 'Abbāsids could establish themselves in Spain, a young Umayyad prince managed to seize power there. This new independent Umayyad state lasted until after 1000, and at times had also a measure of control over North Africa. On its break-up the various regions still in Muslim hands were ruled by local dynasties. Then between 1085 and 1090 a Berber dynasty from North Africa, the Almoravids (al-Murābiṭūn) brought all Muslim Spain under their control. In 1147 they gave place to another Berber dynasty known as the Almohads (al-Muwaḥḥidūn), whose rule in Spain lasted until about 1225. Thereafter the "reconquest" by the Christian states made rapid progress, until little was left except the small state of Granada. This, however, maintained its existence until 1492.

Since Spain was the point at which Islamic culture exerted the greatest influence on that of western Europe, and since the history of Moorish Spain is part of the history of Spain, European scholars have devoted much attention to this portion of the field of Islamic studies.

Most of their attention, however, has been directed to the political history and to the collection and critique of materials for this. If they have studied the writers and thinkers, it has usually been in comparative isolation from their total cultural environment. Thus some important and difficult questions have hardly been asked, far less answered.

The culture of Islamic Spain was continuous with that of the rest of the Islamic world in many important respects. Despite political fragmentation, it was usually possible for Spanish scholars to travel to the main intellectual centres at least as far as Baghdad, and many did so. Sometimes scholars from the east came and settled in Spain. Contributions were made in Spain to the advancement of Islamic humanistic and religious studies. In its greatest periods Moorish culture is reputed to have had a brilliance comparable to that of Baghdad; and even its secular aspects attracted many Christians—those who came to be known as Mozarabs—and induced them to abandon Latin for Arabic. Yet one wonders how much of this brilliance was outward and materialistic. It was certainly the externals of magnificence that first impressed travellers from Christian Europe, which was still in a comparatively barbarous condition. Was there any genuine spiritual vitality, or was the Islamic religion merely the framework of a largely secular way of life? Was there any attempt to adapt the general forms of Islamic culture to the special situation of the Spanish Muslims? Did the traditional culture of the non-Arab Muslims, whether Iberian or Berber, have some influence on the forms of Islamic culture? Until these and similar questions have been answered, it is impossible to give an adequate account of the place of theology and philosophy in the intellectual life of Spanish Islam, and what follows can therefore be no more than a preliminary orientation.

Spain at first followed Damascus in legal and other religious matters, but in course of time the Mālikite rite came to be the dominant one. It is not clear whether this happened by chance or whether Mālikism had some special attraction for the Andalusian temperament. (Al-Andalus was the Arabic name for the whole of Muslim Spain.) Though in the east there was some connection between Mālikite law and Ash'arite theology, there is hardly any trace of Ash'arism in the west before the Almohad movement. The first outstanding theologian of Spain was IBN-ḤAZM (993–1064), sometimes known in the middle ages as Abenhazam. He came of an old (pre-Islamic) Spanish family, and his father was a vizier to the Umayyads. Ibn-Ḥazm himself occupied various administrative and ministerial posts under local rulers in the stormy first quarter of the eleventh century, but eventually retired from political life and devoted himself to scholarship. He was educated under Mālikite teachers, but found this rite unsatisfying. After following the Shāfi'ite rite for some time, he at last found his spiritual home in the minor Ẓāhirite rite.

The essential principle of the Ẓāhirite position was that the statements of the Qur'ān and the Traditions are to be taken in their literal sense; *ẓāhir*, outward or literal, is contrasted with *bāṭin*, inward or esoteric. The previous exponents of this position had applied it only to legal questions, and in theology had adopted several different views. Ibn-Ḥazm now attempted to apply the Ẓāhirite principle to matters of dogma, thus bringing together law and theology in a single intellectual structure. Indeed grammar also was included, as has recently been shown in a careful study of Ibn-Ḥazm by Roger Arnaldez. The chief aim might be said to be to present a view of the whole of human life based solely on the objective divine revelation and excluding everything subjective. This was the coherent elaboration of a religious intuition with deep roots in the Muslim soul—the intuition which finds expression in the traditional view that the Qur'ān was in no way influenced by Muḥammad's personality but was brought to him from outside himself (from God) by an angel. This intuition, and the whole practical attitude of Ibn-Ḥazm is close too to the act which is the climax of Muslim worship—the act of *sujūd* or touching the ground with the forehead in the formal prayers, in total submission of one's humanity to the omnipotence of God. It is therefore not surprising that Ibn-Ḥazm had considerable influence in the Islamic west, even though he had no followers. His theological ideas were not adopted by the Ẓāhirite jurists, and indeed the legal rite disappeared; yet something of his outlook is to be found in many later writers of the region, even when their general position is very different from his.

Ibn-Ḥazm has not presented his theological views in a comprehensive treatise, but in a "critical history of religious ideas" known as *Kitāb al-Fiṣal.* This is in part an Islamic heresiography which gives full reasons for rejecting the heretical views described; but it also deals with other religions, notably Christianity, in the same way. This feature, which led the Spanish Islamist Miguel Asin Palacios, to speak of him as "the first historian of religious ideas", is perhaps due to the conditions of inter-religious contact in Islamic Spain. Ibn-Ḥazm was particularly bitter in his attacks on the Ash'arites and their doctrine of the divine attributes; he regarded as a subjective element their use of "analogical" reasoning in connection with this topic. In some respects he was less harsh with the Mu'tazilites. He was in fact in a difficult position, for he wanted to deny both anthropomorphism and the metaphorical interpretation of the Qur'ānic terms like "hand". The modern scholar is bound to judge that he failed to do what he set out to do. Yet the weaknesses do not impair the grandeur of the positive achievement.

The only other theologian of note in the Islamic west is IBN-TŪMART (*c.* 1080–1130), the founder of the Almohad movement. He was born in North Africa, but went to Cordova about 1107, then after making the pilgrimage to Mecca passed on to Baghdad. Despite stories of his meeting with al-Ghazālī it is practically certain that he never did so; but he came under his influence. While in Spain he probably also came under the influence of Ibn-Ḥazm. He is often spoken of as having spread Ash'arite views in the West, but he is not a consistent Ash'arite, and was apparently chiefly concerned in attacking anthropomorphism. His conception of God seems to depend on philosophy more than on revelation; and it is curious that at this point he agrees with Ibn-Ḥazm in rejecting the Ash'arite view of the attributes of God.

His visit to the East is said to have inspired him with a plan for the reform of the West, so that he began preaching in the boat on his return journey. He had to move from centre to centre, however, as opposition developed. Eventually he found supporters among the Berbers of the Maṣmūda and other tribes, and began an insurrection against the Almoravids, while at the same time proclaiming that he was the Mahdī (about 1121). Though he was defeated by the Almoravids in 1123, the movement had gained many more adherents before his death (probably in 1130), and his successor 'Abd-al-Mu'min was able to destroy the Almoravid power in North Africa in 1147, and then in due course bring Muslim Spain under his control, and even recover some territory from the Christians. The claim to be the Mahdī or "guided leader" is usually referred to as a Shī'ite feature, and it was doubtless suggested by Shī'ite Islam, but its ready acceptance and its importance in the Almohad movement depend on the innate need of the Berbers for a divinely inspired or otherwise superhuman leader—as witnessed by the popular cult of marabouts or holy men. Ibn-Tūmart composed books of instruction for his followers in the Berber language (in which also the call to prayer was given), and spoke of the Almoravids as anthropomorphists and the fighting against them as a *jihād* or holy war. Thus the movement, despite its political successes, had a definite religious basis.

It was during the Almohad period in Spain (which may be dated 1147–1225) that there took place a great flowering of philosophy. This was in large part due to the encouragement or at least toleration of philosophers by the Almohad regime—the doctrines of the founder of the movement, though he was a theologian and not a philosopher, were not far removed from philosophy at some points. There had also been one or two distinguished exponents of philosophy in Spain. It was said to have been introduced by ABENMASARRA (Ibn-Masarra), the son of an immigrant from the East. There are Empedoclean elements in his thought. There was opposition to him from the jurists, and he could not teach publicly but only in an isolated hermitage. He died in 931.

After him no philosopher of note is mentioned for about two hundred years. In Avempace or IBN-BĀJJA (d. 1138) philosophy becomes an ethical protest against the materialistic outlook and the worldliness of the upper classes of the day. The man who has seen the folly and the wrongness of the prevailing attitude must keep himself aloof from it, at least in his thinking. In accordance with this viewpoint he calls his chief work *The Rule of the Solitary*. Although the chief underlying motive was probably this moral one, the conclusions are worked out in terms of a very thorough analysis of the human mind and human thinking, and this analysis has been of great interest and value to subsequent philosophers.

A young admirer of Ibn-Bājja, though, despite the statements of some biographers, probably not an actual pupil, was IBN-ṬUFAYL (*c.* 1105–85). He was known in medieval times as Abubacer from his *kunya* or "father-name" of Abū-Bakr. Born in the small town of Guadix north-east of Granada, he served in various administrative posts and finally became court-physician and vizier of the Almohad prince Abū-Ya'qūb Yūsuf (1163–84). His chief work is the romance of *Ḥayy ibn-Yaqẓān* ("Alive son of Awake"), perhaps the most charming of all philosophical works in Arabic, and reminiscent in some ways of Plato.

The story of Ḥayy is that of a baby cast adrift in a box (or produced by spontaneous generation), who is brought up by a gazelle on an uninhabited island, and who, by the use of his reason, works out a complete philosophical religion for himself, which is crowned by the experience of mystical ecstasy. Eventually there comes to Ḥayy's island a young man called Asāl from a neighbouring island who has been brought up in the traditional religion but is inclined to metaphorical interpretation and to esoteric and spiritual meanings, and who now wants to devote himself entirely in solitude to the worship of God. When he and Ḥayy meet, they find that his spiritualized form of the traditional religion and Ḥayy's philosophical religion are really the same. Asāl tells Ḥayy of the island he has come from, where a friend of his Salāmān is ruler, who follows the literal meaning (*ẓāhir*) and avoids metaphorical interpretation. They go to the inhabited island and Ḥayy tries to instruct the ordinary people in his philosophical religion, but gives up in despair when he finds that their intellects are incapable of understanding it. In the end Ḥayy and Asāl return to the uninhabited island to spend their days in worship.

This is obviously a defence of the position of philosophy in the life of the Almohad state. Ḥayy stands for pure philosophy, Asāl for philosophical theology—possibly for that of Ibn-Tūmart—and Salāmān for that of the ordinary people and probably also of the Mālikite jurists. What is interesting here is the abandonment of the claim of the earlier philosophers like al-Fārābī that philosophy was necessary for the proper ordering of the state. For Ibn-Ṭufayl philosophy is seen to be incapable of directing the lives of the inhabitants of the state. It can lead a few selected individuals to the highest felicity, but to reach this they must retire from active life. In other words the *summum bonum* of the philosopher has become mystical ecstasy.

It is interesting to compare this attitude of Ibn-Ṭufayl with that of his younger friend Averroes or Ibn-Rushd (1126–98). The latter came of a family of jurists, his grandfather being specially well known. He himself also received a legal training, and spent much of his life as judge in Seville and Cordova. He was well versed in the Greek sciences and for a time (in 1182) followed his friend Ibn-Ṭufayl as physician at the Almohad court. The story is told in detail of how he was first introduced by Ibn-Tufayl to the Almohad prince Abū-Yaʿqūb Yūsuf possibly in 1153 (before he came to the throne). The prince asked him whether the philosophers considered the heavens created-in-time or eternal, but out of fear he excused himself and denied his study of philosophy. The prince then turned to the older man and spoke of the views of Plato, Aristotle and other philosophers and of the refutation of them by the theologians; and thereupon Averroes took courage and spoke to him freely, and retained his friendship and support until the prince's death in 1084. His fears were not entirely groundless, for the next sovereign, when the war against the Christian Spaniards was going badly for him and he needed the support of the jurists, had to take mild repressive measures against Averroes, though he subsequently found him a position in his court in Marrakesh.

At the centre alike of the life and of the thought of Averroes is the conviction that philosophy and revelation are both true. He reconciled the two in his life, since he was a judge (rising to be chief qāḍī of Cordova) and a writer on Mālikite law as well as a philosopher. He also gave considerable attention to the intellectual reconciling of the two in his philosophical works. Specially important is the essay known as *Faṣl al-Maqāl*; the full title may be rendered "the decisive treatise, determining the nature of the connection (or harmony) between religion and philosophy"; but in English, following the hint of the latest translator, we might perhaps call it *The Harmony of Religion and Philosophy*. In this essay Averroes bases the discussion on the principles that philosophy is true and that the revealed scriptures are true, and that there cannot therefore be any disharmony between them. Most of the essay then consists in showing how apparent contradictions are to be removed. Philosophy is in general true and unalterable, though there may have been mistakes and misunderstandings in points of detail; and so the work of reconciliation has to be effected chiefly through finding harmonious interpretations of the scriptures.

The closing section of his book *The Inconsistency of the Inconsistency* has a succinct expression of his views on the relation of philosophy and religion. He does not believe that the philosopher should withdraw from active life or eschew popular religion, but that he "should choose the best religion of his period"; it is assumed that this is "the one in which he has been brought up", in short, Islam (though this is not explicitly stated). Because of the importance of religion for the life of the state the philosopher must accept its formulations and explain them. A religion of pure reason Averroes thinks inferior to the revealed religions when philosophically understood. All this shows that he has a full understanding of the place of religion in society and polity, and also in the early training even of the philosopher. He also saw that the class of religious intellectuals would only fulfil their functions adequately when they remained in contact with the ordinary people. He seems further to have held that part of this function was to criticize contemporary society, and he does this very acutely in the course of his commentary on the *Republic* of Plato.

What has just been said is an indication of the place of Averroes in the development of Islamic thought in Spain, but does not touch on his importance in the general history of philosophy. His greatness here rests first and foremost on his work as a commentator of Aristotle. He had a profound knowledge of Aristotelian thought, and in the commentaries he wrote on many of the works he was able to remove some of the Neo-platonic interpretations which had hitherto been current in Arabic. His superlative merits were recognized by the Christian and Jewish scholars then in Spain, and his commentaries were translated into Hebrew and Latin. This was the first main introduction of Aristotle to Europe, and was the seed which led to the flowering of medieval philosophy in Thomism, even if that was in part a reaction to the distortion of Averroes' teaching by the Latin Averroists into the theory of the "double truth".

Another major philosophical work was *The Inconsistency of the Inconsistency* in which he set out to refute what al-Ghazālī had said about philosophy in *The Inconsistency of the Philosophers*. This book, which is now available in an excellent English translation, is a masterly exposition of Averroes' faith in the capacity of reason to attain to a knowledge of the inner secrets of the world. Yet in some respects it was a failure. Averroes had no influence in the Islamic world comparable to his influence in Europe. This was not simply due to the collapse of Islamic civilization in Spain shortly after his death, for his *Inconsistency* at least was known in the East. More important was probably his failure to convince the main body of scholarly opinion in Spain and North Africa that there was a place for philosophy alongside their rather unphilosophical theology. Moreover, though he had written against al-Ghazālī, he had never had to deal with any prominent Ash'arites in the flesh; thus his arguments would be unlikely to convince any Ash'arites, and yet they were the people in the East most sympathetic to philosophy.

By the end of the twelfth century the Almohad hold on Spain was loosening, and after the serious defeat of Navas de Tolosa in 1212 the internal quarrels of the dynasty led to their abandonment of Spain by about 1225. Despite this political crisis and the Christian advance academic studies continued. One well-known name is that of MUḤYĪ-D-DĪN IBN-'ARABĪ (1165–1240); although there are frequent references to his "philosophy", it is rather a theosophy, since he was a mystic with pantheistic tendencies. He went to the east in 1201 on pilgrimage, and remained there for the rest of his life.

A man who, though also a mystic, had a better claim to the title of philosopher was IBN-SAB'ĪN. He must have been born before 1200, since his chief teacher died in 1214. He spent most of his life in Spain or North Africa, but died in Mecca in 1270 by opening his veins. Some attention has been paid to his *Answers to Sicilian Questions* which had been asked of the Muslim scholars in Ceuta by the emperor Frederick II, but their authenticity has been doubted.

The final blaze of glory of the Islamic west is in the work of IBN-KHALDŪN (1332–1406), which may be mentioned here though it properly belongs to the next chapter. His chief importance at the present time is held to be in his pioneer work in sociology, but he is also a great historian. His chapter on theology in his *Muqaddima* or *Introduction* (to his universal history) has been known to European scholars since the publication and translation of that work in the nineteenth century, and also the fact that he wrote a book on logic. Recently an early work of his own on theology has been published which shows his competence in Ash'arite theology; it is essentially a summary of the *Muḥaṣṣal* of Fakhr-ad-Dīn ar-Rāzī. It is worth mentioning here that Ibn-Khaldūn like Averroes, but to a greater extent, had personal experience of high administrative positions. It was doubtless the responsibility of office that gave Averroes his insight into the function of religion in the state; and there is a sense in which the sociological thought of Ibn-Khaldūn is a continuation of this side of the work of Averroes.

BIBLIOGRAPHY

Ignaz GOLDZIHER, *Die Ẓâhiriten, ihr Lehrsystem und ihre Geschichte*, Leipzig, 1884. Pp. 116-70 deal with Ibn-Ḥazm as a theologian.

Roger ARNALDEZ, *Grammaire et théologie chez Ibn Ḥazm de Cordoue: Essai sur la structure et les conditions de la pensée musulmane*, Paris, 1956; a detailed study emphasizing the coherence of the methodological principles.

M. ASIN PALACIOS, *Abenházam de Córdoba y su Historia de las ideas religiosas*, Madrid, 1927, etc.

Ignaz GOLDZIHER, "Materialien zur Kenntniss der Almohadenbewegung", *Zeitschrift der deutschen morgenländischen Gesellschaft*, xli (1887), 30-140. Also *Le Livre de Moḥammed ibn Toumert*, Algiers, 1903 (introduction by Goldziher to a text edited by Luciani). These are still unsurpassed. Cf. also arts. "Ibn Tūmart" (in *EI(S)* by R. Basset); " 'Abd al-Mu'min" (in *EI²* by E. Lévi-Provençal); Robert Brunschwig, "Sur la doctrine du Mahdi Ibn Tūmart", *Ignace Goldziher Memorial Volume* (ed. S. Löwinger), ii. 1-13.

For Ibn-Masarra see *GALS*, i. 378 f.

AVEMPACE, *El régimen del Solitario*, ed. and tr. into Spanish by Miguel Asin Palacios, Madrid, 1946. Engl. tr. of first section by D. M. Dunlop in *Journal of the Royal Asiatic Society*, 1945, 61-81.

English translations of *Ḥayy ibn-Yaqẓān:* (1) *The Improvement of Human Reason*, by S. Ockley, London, 1708; revised by A. S. Fulton, London, 1929; (2) *The Awakening of the Soul*, by P. Brönnle, London (Wisdom of the East Series), 1904. Also edition and French translation by L. Gauthier, Beirut, 1936.

L. GAUTHIER, *Ibn Rochd* (*Averroës*), Paris, 1948; also *Traité décisif* (edition and translation of *Faṣl al-Maqāl*), Algiers, 1942, etc. G. tends to emphasize the rationalism of Averroes.

George F. HOURANI, edition of *Faṣl al-Maqāl*, Leiden, 1959. English translation as *Ibn Rushd* (*Averroes*) *on the Harmony of Religion and Philosophy*, London, 1962.

Simon VAN DEN BERGH, *Averroes' Tahafut al-Tahafut* (*The Incoherence of the Incoherence*), two vols., London, 1954. (Gibb Memorial Series.)

R. ARNALDEZ, "La Pensée religieuse d'Averroes", *Studia Islamica*, vii, viii, x; complements the views of Gauthier.

E. I. J. ROSENTHAL, *Averroes' Commentary on Plato's Republic*, Cambridge, 1956; text of Hebrew translation, and English translation of this. The same author's *Political Thought in Medieval Islam*, Cambridge, 1958, has sections on many of the thinkers dealt with in this survey, but is interested in the development of Greek philosophy and tends to neglect their relation to contemporary Islamic history.

For IBN-SAB'ĪN see the Bibliography of P. J. de Menasce, p. 44.

Part Four

THE PERIOD OF DARKNESS

1250–1900

THE HISTORICAL BACKGROUND

THE period from 1250 to 1900 is divided into two at about the year 1500. In the earlier part there was a strong state in Egypt under the Mamlūks, and this controlled Syria as well. In the east the Mongols continued to rule Transoxiana, and under Timur-Lenk or Tamerlane (1369–1404) spread westwards once more; Persia was added to their dominions, and there were temporary invasions of Iraq and Syria. Between Egypt-Syria and Transoxiana various lesser dynasties maintained a degree of peace over smaller or larger areas. The most important was that of the (Mongol) Īl-Khāns of Persia. Without a caliph Baghdad had become a provincial city —Iraq was a province of Persia—though something of its old cultural life continued until the invasions of Timur when it was practically destroyed. As will have been noticed in previous chapters, however, many centres of Islamic learning had developed in Persia, Central Asia, Afghanistan and India. Thus the vast political upheavals produced less dislocation in intellectual life and in social structure than might have been expected. There were indeed great changes, but surprisingly much managed to survive the storm.

The pattern of the four centuries from 1500 to 1900 is much tidier. Three empires developed. That of the Ottoman Turks, with its capital at Constantinople (from 1453), eventually spread its rule over Syria and Egypt, much of Iraq and most of North Africa, and lasted until the First World War. Persia was united by the Safavid dynasty (Shāh Ismā'īl, 1502–24), and sometimes had parts of Iraq added to it. Baghdad was now on the frontier between these two empires, and changed hands several times. The third empire was that of the Moguls in India, whose real founder was Akbar (1556–1605). It was shorter-lived than the other two; it began to decline before other Indian states about 1700, and then receded as the British East India Company advanced, until it was extinguished in 1857. These empires gave a certain external stability to the Islamic world.

It must also be kept in mind that during the period covered by chapters 16-18 the Islamic religion spread far beyond the lands which had at some time acknowledged a caliph, whether in Damascus, Baghdad or Istanbul. Communities of Muslims were gradually forming in East and West Africa, in Malaya and Indonesia. Colleges were founded—in Timbuctoo and Kano, for example—for the study of Islamic jurisprudence and theology, and a slow islamization of the whole culture began. In the middle of islamization, however, these lands have been struck by the European impact, and it is already certain that, even if Islam comes to dominate their cultures, it will not be in precisely the form in which it has dominated the Middle East. Up to the end of the nineteenth century these peripheral regions, though not contributing any new theological ideas, have helped to swell the volume of theological study.

CHAPTER 16

THE SCLEROSIS OF PHILOSOPHICAL THEOLOGY

WHAT was happening to theological and philosophical thought throughout these centuries? In volume it probably increased, but its quality is usually held to have declined. One of the signs of this alleged decline is the lack of originality. Instead of fresh works like those of al-Juwaynī and Fakhr-ad-Dīn ar-Rāzī, the chief effort of the theologians seems to have gone into the production of commentaries and super-commentaries and glosses on earlier works. One notable instance of this is *The Articles of Belief* of an-Nasafī; for this Brockelmann lists about a dozen commentaries, about thirty glosses (on the commentary by at-Taftazānī), and about twenty super-glosses on one of these. These are mainly in Arabic, but an Islamic religious literature was also springing up in Turkish, Persian, Urdu and other languages. There were a few original works being composed, but these were mainly in the form of creeds of varying lengths, probably intended from the first to be material for commentaries. The writing of commentaries was probably encouraged by the fact that it was the normal practice to use a text as the basis for lectures. Such a practice in itself, however, does not rule out originality. The philosopher Immanuel Kant also followed this practice in his lectures, as was customary in Germany at that period, but this did not prevent him producing highly original work. Apart from the use of the commentary-form, then, originality was lacking.

Gardet and Anawati speak of "rigid conservatism" (*conservatisme figé*).

Before this rigidity is condemned outright, an attempt ought to be made to discover whether it is performing any important social function. After all, the Christian creeds attained a certain fixity about five centuries after the beginnings of Christianity, and there may be some subtle reason for the appearance of a comparable fixity in Islam after the elapse of about the same time. A distinction can be made, however, between the attainment of a definitive creed and rigidity in the interpretation of articles of belief. The problem is therefore whether there is any justification for such theological rigidity as distinct from credal fixity. It is conceivable that in the disturbed political circumstances of the period rigidity in theology helped to give stability to the social structure; perhaps it helped to compensate for the loss of even theoretical unity. It is possible too that the rigidity appears greater to us than it really is, since it is easy for the modern scholar, bored with the repetition of nearly identical arguments whose point he does not appreciate, to transform his own boredom into a characteristic of the material. In the present survey, of course, there is no possibility of saying anything final about this point, since much further study is required.

On the assumption that the period, especially from 1500 onwards was one, not merely of theological rigidity, but of general cultural decline and decadence, theories have been put forward to account for the phenomena on which these judgements are based. One view is that the cause is to be looked for in the Mongol invasions and the devastation they caused. This has certainly much to do with the relative cultural decline of some centres and regions—Baghdad, for example; but Egypt, on the other hand, was never invaded by the Mongols, and therefore the Mongols cannot be the sole cause. Another cause that has been suggested is Ottoman domination. For obvious reasons this tends to be a favourite with modern writers of Arab nationality. There may be some truth in this as regards the Arabic-speaking world, practically all of which came under Ottoman domination; but it is doubtful if even in these regions it can be the whole truth, since Persia and the eastern Islamic lands, where there once had been a high level of culture, never came under Ottoman sway. The further suggestion that the seeds of decay were present in the Islamic religion from the beginning seems to be an expression of anti-Islamic prejudice and not worthy of serious consideration.

Another factor which, though it cannot explain all the phenomena, may yet be of some importance is the extent to which the ulema had become dependent on the governments.[1] The Inquisition of 833 to 849 had made it clear that the class of ulema was ultimately in the power of the government. It was not the brave endurance of Aḥmad ibn-Ḥanbal that brought the Inquisition to an end, but reasons of state quite unconnected with the attitude of the ulema. The basic fact was that the chief appointments in the career to which the ulema might look forward were in the hand of the various governments, and that most of the ulema were too worldly to give up the prospect of a good salary for the sake of religious principle. There were exceptions, such as al-Ghazālī and Ibn-Taymiyya, but the general attitude to the rulers was one of subservience, at least within limits. On the other hand, it must be acknowledged that there was a large field within which the ulema resisted the encroachments of the rulers. Both in jurisprudence and in theology one of the functions of rigidity is probably to strengthen the hands of individuals who are prepared to hold out against some forms of governmental pressure and to prevent a betrayal of the general position of the ulema by individuals who have succumbed to governmental inducements. Where there is a rigid intellectual structure the limits of individual discretion are greatly reduced, and something is undoubtedly thereby attained. Whether this was the best course in the circumstances cannot be decided without much investigation. It is clear, however, that, even if rigidity at some periods had a positive function, it also had disadvantages. In particular it has made it difficult for the ulema to adapt jurisprudence and theology to the needs of recent centuries.

Linked with this dependence of the ulema on the governments is the appearance of a cleavage between them and the common people. In so far as the common people found their religious needs met by the worship of the dervish orders, the official religion presided over by the ulema had failed. There are many unresolved problems here, however. How far was the worship of the orders distinct from that of the Sharīʿa? If distinct, did it replace the latter or was it a complement to it? Was the relation to the common people different in the case of Ḥanbalite theologians and philosophical theologians? The philosophical theologians (whether calling themselves Ashʿarite or not), with their interest in philosophy and their method of commenting on texts, seem to have been largely cut off from the real springs of the spiritual life and restricted to already canalized ideas. Whether the Ḥanbalites were in any better position will be considered in the next section. Despite this apparent weakness of the philosophical theologians, they have a positive achievement to their credit, which should never be forgotten; they preserved a framework of outward conduct and intellectual dogma within which it was possible for men to live lives of moral uprightness and true religious devotion.

It does not appear to be practicable, in the present

condition of the historical studies of this period, to give anything like a survey of the main trends. The best that can be done is to offer brief notes on the best-known theologians, and to warn the reader that there is a vast amount of material that no student of the history of Islamic theology has looked at.

(1) AL-BAYḌĀWĪ (d. 1286) was born near Shiraz in Persia, and apparently ended his life as chief qāḍī there. He had a reputation for piety and asceticism, but his outstanding gift was his ability to select what was best in the works of previous scholars and to summarize it acceptably. His greatest work is his commentary on the Qur'ān which is based mainly on that of az-Zamakhsharī. He was also noted as a theologian, and a comprehensive statement of his views, in about the same compass as al-Ghazālī's *Golden Mean*, has been published in Arabic. The work follows roughly the order of topics in the *Muḥaṣṣal* of Fakhr-ad-Dīn ar-Rāzī, but is if anything more philosophical. In jurisprudence he was a Shāfi'ite.[2]

(2) ḤĀFIẒ-AD-DĪN ABŪ-'L-BARAKĀT AN-NASAFĪ (d. 1301 or 1310) was born near Bukhara and apparently studied there under a teacher who died in 1244. He himself became a teacher, mainly of jurisprudence according to the Ḥanafite rite, in Kirman, a region on the Persian Gulf, and seems to have died on his way back from a visit to Baghdad (which at this period had recovered from the first Mongol invasion). Among his lesser works is *The Pillar of the Creed*, together with a commentary on it. Its doctrines are very similar to those of *The Articles of Belief* by Najm-ad-Dīn an-Nasafī, but it is about four times the length. It is noteworthy, however, that it says less about epistemology than the shorter creed, but the author may have felt that philosophical discussions were out of place in a creed.[3]

(3) AL-ĪJĪ, with the honorific title 'Aḍud-ad-Dīn,

was born near Shiraz after 1280, and educated there under a pupil of a pupil of al-Bayḍāwī. This gives some evidence for the continuity of Shāfiʿite and Ashʿarite learning in Shiraz. Most of his life is said to have been spent as a judge in the recently built capital of the Īl-Khāns, Sultaniyya; but in his latter years he was again in the neighbourhood of Shiraz. Unfortunately he became embroiled with a local governor who was in process of attaining a position of semi-independence, and died in prison in 1355. In theology he is known chiefly for two works. One is the *Mawāqif* or *Stations*, a comprehensive work arranged in roughly the same way as the *Muḥaṣṣal* of ar-Rāzī, but devoting more space to the philosophical preliminaries—two-thirds as against a half. The other work is a creed, usually known as the *ʿAḍudiyya*, which is quite short and has nothing corresponding to the philosophical part of the *Mawāqif*.[4]

(4) AT-TAFTAZĀNĪ (1322–1389 or 1390) was born in Khorasan and is said to have been a pupil of al-Ījī. We hear of him at Herat, and also at one of the minor Mongol courts. When this whole region came under Timur-Lenk, at-Taftazānī was stationed for a time at Sarakhs in the centre of Khorasan, and then moved to the court at Samarqand. He is best known for his commentary on *The Articles of Belief* by Najm-ad-Dīn an-Nasafī, which for centuries was one of the chief textbooks of theology. The curious thing about this is that, though the creed is Māturīdite, at-Taftazānī is usually held to have been an Ashʿarite. The reason is probably that he taught in a region where Māturīdite views were dominant. He expresses himself carefully, but there are a number of points where it is clear that he disagreed with the text he was commenting on.[5]

(5) AL-JURJĀNĪ, known as as-Sayyid ash-Sharīf (1340–1413), was born in Gurgan at the south-east corner of the Caspian Sea, and studied in Herat, in Kir-

man (on the Persian Gulf) and in Egypt, besides visiting Constantinople. He was a friend of at-Taftazānī, and through the latter obtained a professorship in Shiraz about 1377. After the conquest of Shiraz he went to Timur-Lenk's court at Samarqand, and in a celebrated debate showed himself superior to at-Taftazānī. He returned to Shiraz after Timur's death in 1405. Many works in many fields of study were produced by him. Theologically the most important was his commentary on the *Mawāqif* of al-Ījī, where his interest in philosophical questions was given full scope.

(6) As-Sanūsī (d. 1486 or 1490, aged sixty-three) was born at Tlemsen in the west of Algeria, and spent most of his life there. Among his teachers was at least one who had studied and taught in Granada, and who abandoned it as the prospects for the Muslims there became gloomy. He is reckoned an Ash'arite in theology, and was also a sufi; but first and foremost he is a philosopher. The work which has attracted most attention is a short creed often called the Sanūsiyya, which has been popular with African Muslims, and has also been translated into French and German. It is much more philosophical than the short creed of al-Ījī, and begins, for example, by asserting that every believer must know twenty attributes necessary in respect of God and twenty attributes impossible for him; since among the twenty attributes necessary for God are seven "attributes of forms" which have to be distinguished from seven very similar "attributes pertaining to forms", it is clear that the average believer is expected to be a philosopher.[6] (This theologian must be distinguished from Sīdī-Muḥammad ibn-'Alī as-Sanūsī, d. 1859, the founder of the Sanūsiyya order and ancestor of the reigning dynasty of Libya.)

(7) Ad-Dawwānī (or ad-Dawānī) (1427–1501) came from a district some fifty miles west of Shiraz, and

became a judge and professor in the latter city. Numerous works are extant on philosophical, theological and mystical subjects, including commentaries on some of the works mentioned above, such as those of al-Ijī and al-Jurjānī. There was perhaps a certain local piety in the continued study of these works at Shiraz. The curious thing about ad-Dawwānī is that he is said to have become an Imāmite Shī'ite; but he certainly began as an Ash'arite, witness his commentary on the creed of al-Ījī (article on the imamate of Abū-Bakr), and the work of Naṣīr-ad-Dīn aṭ-Ṭūsī commented on by him is philosophical and has nothing of Shī'ite dogmatics.

(8) Birgevi, or Birgili (1522–73) was a Turkish scholar from north-west Asia Minor. He completed his education in Istanbul, and eventually taught at a college at the little town of Birgi in the province of Smyrna. He stood boldly for the strict and faithful observance of the Sharī'a, and considered, for example, that it was wrong to teach the Qur'ān for money. His unswerving rectitude and the popularity of his preaching gained him a numerous following among the common people. A creed or statement in Turkish of the principles of religion achieved a wide circulation and had commentaries written on it,[7] but he himself, like many Turks, was largely unphilosophical.

(9) Al-Laqānī (d. 1631) was a professor at al-Az'har college in Cairo, and belonged to the Mālikite legal rite. He is remembered for a creed in verse called *The Jewel* (*Al-Jaw'hara*), which has been the basis of some well-known commentaries. One such was by his son 'Abd-as-Salām al-Laqānī (d. 1668), who was also a professor at al-Az'har. *The Jewel* is somewhat similar in form to the short creed of as-Sanūsī.[8]

(10) As-Siyālkūtī (d. 1657), the man from Sialcot, was an adviser at the court of the Mogul emperor Shah-Jehan (1628–58). He wrote commentaries and

glosses on some of the theological works regularly studied in Persia and Egypt, and his writings were so highly thought of that they themselves came to be used as textbooks.

(11) AL-FAḌĀLĪ (or -Fuḍālī or -Faḍḍālī) was a native of the Delta and professor at al-Az'har in Cairo, who died in 1821. He wrote an exposition of the Islamic faith of medium length which was translated into English by D. B. Macdonald (as an Appendix to his *Development*).

(12) AL-BĀJŪRĪ (1783–1860), also called al-Bayjūrī, from the Egyptian province of Menouf, became a professor at al-Az'har and latterly rector. Like al-Faḍālī who was one of his teachers he was a Shāfi'ite in law. He was outstanding in his day, but his work consisted mainly in commentaries and glosses, including commentaries on the shorter creed of as-Sanūsī and the exposition just mentioned of al-Faḍālī, as well as a gloss on a commentary on the *Jewel* of al-Laqānī.[9]

These brief notes are far from being a history of theology during this period; yet they give glimpses of what was happening. The "international" character of the discipline is noteworthy, though the scholars move about less than in the centuries before 1258. In spite of the less extensive travelling of scholars, however, important works seem to be known throughout the Sunnite world, and even to some extent among Shī'ites.

BIBLIOGRAPHY

R. BRUNSCHVIG and G. E. VON GRUNEBAUM, *Classicisme et déclin culturel dans l'histoire de l'Islam*, Paris, 1957. Papers read at a symposium at Bordeaux in 1956, the most relevant being those by Louis Gardet, H. S. Nyberg, H. Ritter, G.-H. Bousquet, Fr. Meier, R. Arnaldez.

W. F. THOMPSON, *Practical Philosophy of the Mohammedan People*, London, 1839; translation of the *Akhlāq-i Jalāli* of ad-Dawwānī.

Sir H. A. R. GIBB and H. BOWEN, *Islamic Society and the West*, vol. 1, part 2, London, 1957; deals with a number of topics relevant to this section, in connection with the Ottoman empire.

CHAPTER 17

THE VITALITY OF THE ḤANBALITES

THERE had been vigour, even if tinged with fanaticism, among the Ḥanbalites in Baghdad in the eleventh century; and at that period Baghdad seems to have been their main centre. Before the end of the century, however, there were Ḥanbalite schools in Jerusalem and Damascus; and these eventually came to be concentrated in Damascus when the jurists of Jerusalem had to flee before the Crusaders (who captured Jerusalem in 1099). The Ḥanbalites of Damascus were further strengthened when fresh refugees began to arrive as the Mongols moved westwards into Iraq. Among the refugees was a family from Ḥarrān which included several scholars. One of these, born in January 1263, came to Damascus with his father as a boy of about five, and received a thorough education in the Ḥanbalite schools there. This was IBN-TAYMIYYA (more fully Taqī-'d-Dīn Aḥmad ibn-Taymiyya) who became one of the greatest religious leaders of Islam. Much light has recently been thrown upon his thought and achievement by the studies of Henri Laoust and his collaborators, so that, in contrast to the obscurity around, he stands in a blaze of illumination.[10]

The career of Ibn-Taymiyya is best understood when his primary problem is considered to be the same as that of al-Ghazālī, namely, the corruption of the ulema or religious intellectuals. As a class they were nearly all mainly interested in their own worldly promotion; and, since promotion was in the hands of the rulers, they were subservient to the rulers. Ibn-Taymiyya, following in the tradition of Ibn-Ḥanbal, stood for what he believed to be right, regardless of the suffering it might bring upon him personally. As a result of his intellectual brilliance he is said to have been in a position to give formal legal opinions at the age of seventeen. When he was about twenty-seven by Islamic reckoning (in Dec. 1298), his public troubles began. In response to a request from the people of Hama for instruction on the question of the attributes of God and their relation to his essence, he drew up a statement of his dogmatic position (known as the *Large Creed of Hama*). Enemies, annoyed at his attack on astrology and jealous of his position at the court of the governor of Damascus, made this creed the basis of an attack on Ibn-Taymiyya for the heresy of anthropomorphism. The Shāfiʿite qāḍī of Damascus was involved. The enemies of Ibn-Taymiyya went too far, however, when they got a crier to parade the town proclaiming his heresy; and the governor intervened to preserve order. The jurists were made to examine the creed carefully, and had to report that there was nothing objectionable in it. Thus the incident was closed.

In the succeeding years he took a share in the public life of Damascus, was a member of diplomatic missions, and joined an expedition against revolted Nuṣayrite heretics. After the conquest of the territory of the Nuṣayrites he was consulted by the sultan on their treatment. About the end of 1305, however, he once again found himself in trouble. He publicly attacked the sufi order of the Aḥmadites for engaging in various practices which were contrary to the Sharīʿa. Damascus was at this time part of the Mamlūk state with capital at Cairo, and the head of the Aḥmadites there was on friendly terms with several influential persons. Early in 1306 Ibn-Taymiyya found himself summoned to Cairo. There after a short trial of dubious validity he was imprisoned, and kept in prison until September 1307. On his release he set up as a professor and gave lectures, but his attacks on the pantheism of many of the sufis soon brought him into prison again, first in Cairo and later in Alexandria, since in the latter place his freedom to receive visits would be less dangerous. A change of government brought his release in March 1310, but there was much hostility to him and after nearly two years in Cairo he returned to Damascus.

The remainder of his life he spent in Damascus, generally held in honour and respect, and with many pupils and other followers. On the whole he was less implicated in public incidents, but his attack on the cult of the saints led to his imprisonment in the citadel in July 1326, together with some persecution of his followers, and he continued a prisoner until his death in September 1328.

Laoust conceives the thought of Ibn-Taymiyya as having its climax in a "political sociology"; but this is based on a theological position. The central point of this he sees in the development of the old Islamic idea of the absolute dissimilarity of God and man. From this Ibn-Taymiyya concludes to the impossibility of attaining knowledge of God by rational methods, whether those of philosophy or of philosophical theology, and also to the impossibility of the mystical aim of union with God. This was no mere obscurantism, for Ibn-Taymiyya had made a careful study of the main Arabic philosophers, as well as of theologians like al-Ghazālī and Fakhr-ad-Dīn ar-Rāzī. His criticisms of the philosophers are extremely acute and well founded, notably his *Refutation of the Logicians*. To ar-Rāzī he was strongly opposed because he brought so many foreign elements into theology from philosophy and other sources; but in the general direction of his thought he was influenced by ar-Rāzī, even if only by way of reaction. From al-Ghazālī, to whom he was more sympathetic, he seems to have learnt much.

His attitude to mysticism is complex. He rejects everything resembling "union with God" as the highest aim for human life. Absorption into the One or even contemplation of the highest Good he felt to be at variance with the Sharī'a. For him the highest aim was the worship or service of God (*'ibāda*), whose basis was the observance of the prescriptions of the Sharī'a. Yet in his own make-up there was something of the mystic; and from the standpoint of this conception of "service" he proceeded to give a meaning to many of the terms employed by the sufis—fear of God, confidence in him, humility, love for him. In the perfect fulfilment of the Sharī'a he even found an equivalent annihilation (*fanā'*) to that of which the sufis spoke.

His attacks on saint-worship were linked up with his insistence on adhering to the original forms of Islam, just as his attacks on philosophical conceptions were linked up with his rejection of foreign elements. All this grew out of a realization that the concrete, "poetical" language of the Qur'ān kept men closer to the deep springs of religious vitality than the abstractions of philosophical thinking. From an early period of his life he must have had spiritual experiences of sufficient profundity to give him confidence to adopt an independent and critical attitude towards his teachers and text-books. For himself he had undoubtedly found the source of real life and power in simple (though by no means naïve) acceptance of Islamic dogma and its elaboration in the Qur'ān, and in constant meditation on this, accompanied by the effort to bring his life into accord with his beliefs. Something of this, too, he managed to convey to his followers. Yet the difference between them and the philosophical theologians is not so very great; and it would therefore seem that it was not merely the adulteration of theology with philosophy which led to the theological decline. Perhaps the scholastic method with its rigidity and reliance on "authorities" —and in this the Ḥanbalites shared—had also its contribution to make.

Even if he did not produce outstanding disciples who fully shared his independence of mind, Ibn-Taymiyya has profoundly altered the course of theological thought in Islam, and his influence is still pregnant for the future. He had the advantage of living at a period when Cairo was becoming one of the cultural foci of Islam in place of Baghdad. Cairo was the capital of the relatively stable state of the Mamlūks, which escaped the Mongol invasions; and in Cairo resided the man who in name at least (though he had no power at all) was the Sunnite caliph. Damascus as the second centre of the Mamlūk state was also growing in importance. The reputation of Ibn-Taymiyya and the number of his disciples thus ensured that Ḥanbalism was well represented in the new phase of Islamic thought brought about by this transference. Ḥanbalism here gained a base—or should we say a beach-head?—from which it was able to influence later centuries.

The names are known of many Ḥanbalites scattered through the following centuries, not only in Damascus, but also in Baghdad, Jerusalem and Cairo, who were either explicit followers of Ibn-Taymiyya or at least his admirers and to some extent under his influence. The only one that need be mentioned here is IBN-QAYYIM-AL-JAWZIYYA (1292–1350), whose usual name means "the son of the *qayyim*—perhaps a minor administrative officer—of the Jawziyya college". He became a close follower of Ibn-Taymiyya soon after the master's return from Egypt in 1312, and was thought sufficiently important to be imprisoned in the citadel at the same time as Ibn-Taymiyya, though separately from him. He shared the master's views except that he was also something of a mystic, and he is sometimes thought to have altered Ibn-Taymiyya's later works—he was a kind of literary executor—not only in language but also in sentiment. Undoubtedly, however, both by transmitting the works of the master and by publicizing his ideas in a faultless style in his own works, he did much to spread and perpetuate the influence of Ibn-Taymiyya.

The vitality imparted to Ḥanbalism by Ibn-Taymiyya led to the appearance in the eighteenth century of the Wahhābite movement. The theological founder of this movement, Muḥammad ibn-ʿAbd-al-Wahhāb (1703–92), came, like many other theologians, from a family which had already produced many scholars who had held posts in various small towns in Nejd or Central Arabia. After preliminary studies under his father and in Mecca, he spent some time in Medina as a student, and later went also to Basra in quest of knowledge. From an early age he was aware of the decadence of popular religion in Arabia and of the need for thoroughgoing reform. His first attempts at reform, on his return to Arabia, met with opposition, but in 1744 he was able to make an agreement with the emir (belonging to the family of Suʿūd) of the small town of Darʿiyya. The dynasty of Suʿūd prospered enormously, and in the opening years of the nineteenth century, when they were already rulers of much of Arabia, also occupied Mecca and Medina. But the occupation of the holy cities by the Wahhābites disturbed many Sunnites, and on the instructions of the Ottoman sultan an Egyptian army invaded Arabia (1813–18) and put an end to the Suʿūdite principality for the time being. Through the dynasty's vicissitudes of fortune up to the establishment of the kingdom of Saudi (or Suʿūdī) Arabia in 1930 the association with Wahhābism remained, and the kingdom is still essentially a Wahhābite state.

The theology of the Wahhābites has been described by Laoust (p. 514) as "a fresh edition of Ḥanbalite doctrines and of the prudent agnosticism of the traditional faith". Its clearest dependence on Ibn-Taymiyya is in its attack on the cult of saints and its general insistence on a return to the purity of original Islam. For the most part it is concerned largely with externals, like much of Islamic religious thought. It shows no interest in the methodology of Ibn-Taymiyya, which he devised in order to escape from the rigidity of the scholastic methods and to make possible an adaptation of Islamic truth to contemporary conditions. Much the same is true of the so-called Wahhābites of India, who appeared in the early nineteenth century, stimulated by an armed movement under Sayyid Aḥmad (1786–1831) against the Sikhs and the British. In origins the movement was due to internal Indian causes, but in 1823 Sayyid Aḥmad came under Wahhābite influence while on the pilgrimage to Mecca. Something of the Wahhābite spirit has been retained in the important theological seminary at Deoband.

Thus the upsurge of vitality in Ḥanbalism in the person of Ibn-Taymiyya continues down to the present time. His insistence on maintaining or returning to the purity of original Islam points out to the Islamic thinkers of today, whether professional theologians or not, the surest way of finding a solution to their problems. Among the Egyptian modernists this has been realized most fully by M. Rashīd Riḍā (d. 1935), who was an admirer of Ibn-Taymiyya and in particular of his methodology.

Bibliography

Henri Laoust, *Essai sur les doctrines sociales et politiques de Taḳī-d-Dīn Aḥmad b. Taimīya*, Cairo,

1939; one of the most important works on Islamic theology published this century, since it opens up a virgin field; it contains chapters on the transmission of his doctrines by later Ḥanbalites, on Muḥammad ibn-ʿAbd-al-Wahhāb and the Wahhābite theocracy, and on the Egyptian reform movements under Muḥammad ʿAbduh and Rashīd Riḍā.

D. S. MARGOLIOUTH, art. "Wahhābīya", in *EI*[1].

CHAPTER 18

THE TRANSFORMATION OF SHĪʿISM

In the period between 1258 and 1900 the two main forms of Shīʿism, the Imāmite and the Ismāʿīlite, underwent a complete transformation. This was not in respect of their main dogmatic position but in respect of their function in the life of the Islamic community as a whole.

In the case of the Imāmites the change came about suddenly in the year 1502. Until that time the Imāmites were simply a theological party intermingled with the Sunnites in a single community of Muslims. There were towns where the Imāmites were dominant, and other areas where they were hardly represented at all; but on the whole it is correct to say that the Imāmites and the Sunnites were living side by side. It has already been noted that at least some of their theologians were in the mainstream of Islamic thought, certainly being influenced by it and perhaps also to a slight extent influencing it. It is therefore not surprising that in the period now being considered Imāmite theology shows many of the features of Sunnite theology—the composition of short creeds and the writing of lengthy commentaries on them, and the introduction of much philosophy into theology.

The most outstanding Imāmite thinker of the thirteenth century was Naṣīr-ad-Dīn aṭ-Ṭūsī (1201–1274). He has also some connections with Ismāʿīlism, for prior to 1256 he was for a number of years an official in the service of the Ismāʿīlite ruler of Qūhistān (a region to the south-west of Khurasan in eastern Persia) and then subsequently resided at the Ismāʿīlite "capital", the fortress of Alamut (north of Teheran). His relation to the Ismāʿīlites is not clear. He may have had some sympathy with their views, and on the other hand Alamut in its closing years (cf. *EI*²) had the reputation of cultivating "a broad Islamic outlook". He is accused, however, of advising the Ismāʿīlite leader to surrender Alamut to the Mongols in 1256—and the surrender was followed by the execution of the leader and the massacre of his followers. Yet this, like the story that he advised Hulagu, the Mongol general, to put the ʿAbbāsid caliph to death in 1258, may be a libel of his opponents. What is certain is that before 1258 he had gained the favour of Hulagu, and that for the rest of his life he held various high appointments in the Mongol administration. This may have been due in part to his skill as an astrologer, since the Mongols seem to have consulted him about auspicious dates for important occasions.

Naṣīr-ad-Dīn aṭ-Ṭūsī was more a philosopher than a theologian. Indeed he was well versed in all the Greek sciences, especially in mathematics and astronomy. His philosophy, of course, was not the pure philosophy of an Avicenna, but was ostensibly a preliminary to theology. He lived in much the same world of thought as Fakhr-ad-Dīn ar-Rāzī (d. 1209), on whose *Muḥaṣṣal* he composed a commentary, largely positive and expository, but where necessary showing his disagreements. This and other of his works were freely studied by philosophically minded Sunnite theologians.

The only other Imāmite who need be mentioned in the period up to 1500 is a pupil of Naṣīr-ad-Dīn called Ibn-al-Muṭahhar al-Ḥillī, known as ʿAllāma-i-Ḥillī (1250–1325). Ḥilla, some sixty miles south of Baghdad, was an important Imāmite centre for centuries, and produced many noted scholars. Ibn-al-Muṭahhar was probably the most distinguished

Imāmite scholar of his day. A work of his on the methodology of law came into the hands of Ibn-Taymiyya in Damascus and influenced him considerably; in part he reacted against it, but he also seems to have been impressed by the possibility of the jurist judging questions independently (*ijtihād*) and to have accepted something of this conception into his own thinking.[11] Ibn-al-Muṭahhar does not appear to have been much interested in the more philosophical aspects of theology, though he made use of certain philosophical conceptions. A short creed of his—the "eleventh chapter" of a longer work—has been translated into English, along with a commentary of the fifteenth century, under the title *Al-Bābu 'l-Hādī ʿAshar.*

The transformation of the Imāmite sect took place in 1502 when Shah Ismāʿīl, the founder of the Safavid dynasty, at the same time as he was crowned king of Persia in Tabriz, took steps to have Imāmite Shīʿism made the official religion of his realm. He had still much of Persia to conquer, but that he rapidly achieved. With the impetus derived from his political successes the Imāmite faith became not merely the state religion but in effect the only tolerated religion. There are reports of an initial scarcity of religious teachers, since Shīʿism was by no means the dominant religion of the Persians at this time; in Tabriz, for example, two-thirds of the population are reported to have been Sunnites. From what has been said earlier it is clear that Imāmite teaching and Imāmite scholars were in principle available in the fields of both law and theology, but there may easily have been temporary shortages, since many Imāmite centres were outside Persia—at Ḥilla, Bahrein and Mount Amila (in the Lebanon), for example.

One of the main differences between Imāmite and Sunnite jurisprudence is that among the Imāmites duly qualified jurists give decisions that are based directly (that is, by their own arguments) on the general principles contained in Qur'ān and Tradition, whereas among the Sunnites by this time even the most learned jurist had to base his decisions on the decisions of earlier jurists. The giving of independent decisions was known as *ijtihād*, and the person qualified to do this was a *mujtahid*. The Sunnite position was expressed by saying that "the gate of *ijtihād* was closed". This belief in the continuing right of *ijtihād* must have helped in the adaptation of the existing legal system to the needs of the new state, but the intellectual development of Imāmite Persia has not been adequately studied. One thing that has been recorded is a split within the Imāmites over this matter of *ijtihād*. Muḥammad Amīn al-Astarābādhī (d. 1624) is held to be the leader of the attack on the *mujtahids* and those who believed in *ijtihād*, and the founder of a subdivision of the Imāmites known as the AKHBĀRITES ("Traditionists").[12] Their view was that legal opinions should be based on Traditions (*akhbār*) only, and not derived from general principles (*uṣūl*) by analogical reasoning or otherwise. This sub-sect looks like a Shī'ite form of Ḥanbalism, and one wonders whether its appearance is due to the forcible incorporation of men of Ḥanbalite sympathies into the Imāmite state. Those who retained the more usual Imāmite view came to be known as Uṣūlites and Mujtahidites. The Akhbārites after a short period of activity seem to have dwindled away and disappeared.

Another deviant group in an opposite direction were the SHAYKHITES. These were the followers of Shaykh Aḥmad al-Aḥsā'ī (1744–1827).[13] His views contained a large admixture of philosophy, but what they meant in the contemporary situation is not clear. He was influenced by an earlier philosopher, Mullā Ṣadrā, who was interested in mysticism also and who died about 1660. The theosophical strain in the Shaykhites was further developed about the middle of the nineteenth century into Bābism and Bahā'ism. Though these began as sectarian movements within the Islamic community, they have developed into separate religions and are therefore outside the range of this survey.[14]

The Ismāʿīlite branch of Shīʿism may be dealt with more briefly. The fall of Alamut to the Mongols in 1256 was followed by massacres, but many Ismāʿīlites survived and the son of the last imam was preserved safely in hiding. The subsequent history is complex and known only in general outline, but since it is political rather than theological it will not be necessary here to go into detail. The division mentioned earlier into the followers of al-Mustaʿlī and the followers of Nizār has persisted, and each branch has become further subdivided, though several of the subdivisions are now of little importance. The Mustaʿlians disappeared from Egypt and came to have their main base first in the Yemen and later in Gujarat. The Nizārites, though maintaining themselves in Syria and Persia eventually also came to be strongest in India (where Ismāʿīlite propaganda had begun in the ninth century). The main body of the Nizārites is the community which has as its head the Aga Khan. It is strong in India, East Africa and elsewhere. Perhaps the most interesting thing about it is the way in which what was once the faith of rebellious mountaineers has become that of a closely knit and prosperous community of merchants and men in other urban or industrial occupations, which in many respects presents other Muslims with an example worthy of study of the Islamic faith in effective action in the modern world.

Bibliography

R. Strothmann, art. "Shīʿa" in *EI(S)*: also *Die Zwölfer-Schīʿa*, Leipzig, 1926.

E. G. BROWNE, *A Literary History of Persia*, Cambridge, 1924, etc. iv. 353-411; deals with Shīʿite theology from its beginnings.

Cl. HUART, art. "Shaikhī" in *EI*¹.

W. IVANOW, art. "Ismāʿīlīya" in *EI(S)*; also edition and translation of the *True Meaning of Religion*, by Shihāb-ad-Dīn Shāh (son of the 47th imam of the Nizārites), Bombay, 1933.

M. HORTEN, *Die Gottesbeweise bei Schirazi*, Bonn, 1912; *Das philosophische System von Schirazi*, Strasburg, 1913; "Die philosophischen und theologischen Ansichten von Lahīgi (*c.* 1670)", *Der Islam*, iii (1912), 91-131. These works give some idea of developments in Persia, especially through the introduction and index to the third. The second has a useful glossary. "Schirazi" is the person referred to in the chapter as Mullā Ṣadrā.

Henry CORBIN, "Pour une morphologie de la Spiritualité Shīʿite", *Eranos-jahrbuch*, xxix (1960), 57-107; has a section (pp. 71-81) on Shaykhism, and is in general of much interest.

John Kingsley BIRGE, *The Bektashi Order of Dervishes*, London, 1937; may be given as an illustration of how Shīʿism tended towards pantheism.

Part Five

THE NEW DAWN

CHAPTER 19

THE PROSPECT FOR THEOLOGY

THE last three chapters have not been a complete account of the development of Islamic thought in the period up to 1900, since signs of the "new dawn" appearing before 1900 were not mentioned. This phrase is here being used to indicate the response of Islamic thought, and of theology in particular, to the challenge presented by the European impact. No attempt will be made, however, to give a detailed description of this new dawn in all its many aspects, since another volume in this series is to be devoted to the subject. The aim of this brief concluding chapter is simply to give a general picture of the problems now confronting Islamic theology. Philosophy need not be considered separately, since there are now no "bearers" of Islamic philosophy apart from the theologians.

In so far as modern European culture is an expression of the Greek spirit, the impact of Europe on the Islamic world might be called "the third wave of Hellenism". Such a conception, however, would tend to obscure important differences between the present situation and those referred to as the first two waves. In the previous cases the impact was mainly intellectual, though the bearers of the alien intellectual culture were mixed with the Muslim inhabitants of the caliphate. The present impact of Europe, on the other hand, has been much more than intellectual. It began with commercial dealings in the easterly regions of the Islamic world after the discovery of the route to India by Vasco da Gama in 1498. Commerce eventually led to political interference and then to political domination. With the expedition of Napoleon to Egypt in 1798 the Ottoman and Persian empires began to feel the full impact of Europe. Commercial and political penetration were now supported by financial operations. It is hardly too much to say that when the new educated classes in the various Islamic countries came to an awareness of their position in the modern world they were already inextricably entangled in the web of international finance. Extended visits to Europe by students, translations of European books, and American and European films meant close contacts with an alien social structure and way of life; and one of the results of this is the movement for improving the position of women.

It is also important to notice the precise form of the intellectual impact. In the independent Islamic countries the demand for European education usually arose out of a realization by the rulers of their military inferiority. In order to have an army on the European model they had to have a measure of European education for their officers. From such beginnings there grew a complete system of Western education, stretching from primary schools to universities. While this was happening in the "secular" sphere, the religious leaders showed no interest whatsoever in the new education. The old educational system continued alongside the new, with its Qur'ān-schools in the villages and its traditional-type universities like al-Azhar in Cairo. The result of having two educational systems functioning side by side has been to create two distinct classes of intellectuals—the ulema or old-fashioned religious intellectuals, and the new Western-educated intellectuals. Both of these, moreover, are largely cut off from the common people, the ulema because of their excessive philosophizing and because of the rigidity which prevented adaptation to changing conditions, and the moderns because they had become almost completely Western in their outlook.

It is in the practical sphere first of all that the ulema have become alive to the need for reform, and they have devised various methods or stratagems for bringing the legal practice of Islamic countries more into line with the general world outlook. On the intellectual side they have been much slower. Until after the Second World War hardly any of the ulema in Egypt, for example, could read books in a European language. Thus their ideas of the modern world were derived at best from a limited number of translations or from the secular writings of Arabs who stood in the European tradition. This was all their equipment for dealing with the intellectual problems of young Muslims who had been studying science in Europe and reading the works of scientific humanists. To make matters worse the traditional suspicion of Christianity among Muslims has led these young students to prefer the humanistic and anti-religious European writers. In this predicament we find some of the ulema turning to "heretical" Arabic philosophers like Avicenna and Averroes; but it is a gesture of despair.

Where is the Muslim of today, inescapably bound to this situation, to look for intellectual renewal? What is needed is a set of ideas which is both a development of traditional theological conceptions and also relevant to contemporary problems; and this relevance really implies that intellectual renewal and social reform must go hand in hand. Where is this set of ideas to be found? Who is to produce it? The ulema are unlikely to do so, because they are insufficiently familiar with European ideas and therefore unable to communicate easily with the modern-minded politicians who have the actual power. The modern intellectuals are likewise incapable of producing a suitable set of ideas; they tend to think in European conceptions (including Marxist), and, though they are able to speak to the politicians, they are unable to link up with the traditional categories of Islamic thinking, and thus cannot carry the religious leaders and the masses with them.

The situation varies, of course, in the different countries. Turkey is at one extreme, in that it has turned away from Islamic ideas and officially accepted a Western outlook. If the present attempts to revive Islamic theology in Turkey are successful, the results should be most important. Pakistan is also interesting, since it has had a longer effective contact with Europe than a Middle-Eastern country like Egypt, and its reactions therefore tend to be more mature. There are also features of interest in Tunisia, Egypt, Syria and Iraq. It is from these countries that intellectual renewal is most likely to come, and not from the peripheral ones and the less advanced. The situation in Persia is similar to that elsewhere, but it is difficult for it to help the other countries much since it is officially Shīʿite, and therefore in many ways cut off from them.

There have, of course, been numerous attempts to deal with the problem, or part of it, from various angles. The most noteworthy of these have been by men whose field was literature and not theology. One of the oldest of these (and one that is easily accessible) is *The Spirit of Islam*, by Syed Ameer Ali (revised edition, London, 1922). In the strictly theological field the most important contribution has been that of the Egyptian Muḥammad ʿAbduh (1849–1905). Besides producing the first "modernistic" work of theology, he inaugurated the long work of reforming the university of al-Azhar. In both spheres he may appear to have achieved little, but the important thing was that the current had begun to flow in another direction. The intellectual product which comes nearest to the set of ideas desiderated above is to be found in the poems of Sir MUḤAMMAD IQBĀL (1876–1938) and his *Reconstruction of Religious Thought in Islam* (lectures first delivered in 1928). Though he did not live to see the independent Muslim state of Pakistan (and might not have approved of it), he is regarded as its spiritual founder; and it may be that the balance of the traditional and the modern in it is largely due to his influence.

Out of all this ferment something may yet come. It is far too soon to pronounce the position hopeless. A man with the requisite training, and above all with gifts of courage and wisdom, might transform the whole scene. It is practically certain that he would meet with fierce criticism from his colleagues, and would have to stand firm. His opponents might also have resort to violence. He would therefore have to have sufficient personal magnetism to gain the support of the masses and of a proportion of the *élite*. Where is such a man to be found? Reasons can be given to show that no Islamic *milieu* is likely to produce him; but he may nevertheless appear.

So far the discussion has been in terms of the intellectual impact of Europe on the Islamic world, and in particular of European scientific and secular thought. A distinct though minor facet of this has been the Christian missionary movement in Islamic lands. There have been "replies" to Christian propaganda and criticism of Christian activities—probably only of ephemeral importance. In recent years, however, there have been some discussions of Christian themes by Muslim men of letters—notably *City of Wrong*, by Kamel Hussein, translated by Kenneth Cragg (London, Amsterdam, 1960)—and these may perhaps prepare the way for completely new initiatives in Islamic theology.

Quite separate from the problems created by the intellectual impact is the emergent problem of what is sometimes called "inter-religion". This is the problem created by modern means of communication—fast travel for all, and the global reach of broadcasting. Each of the great religious communities—and the quasi-religion of Marxism might be included—is in closer contact with the other great religions than has ever been the case before. Members of the great religions are being forced, as never before, to learn how to live alongside adherents of other faiths. Consequently there are strong pressures urging men towards a unified world religion. Ideally all that is of value in the several religions should be taken up into this one religion; but it is possible that to begin with humanity may fall far short of this ideal, and in this way much of value may be lost. The new problem for Islamic theologians, as for those of all the religions (including Christianity) is to present what they see of value in their religion in such a form that it is capable of being assimilated by others. The present survey has been written from the standpoint that there is much of value in Islam; and it would thus be a loss for the whole world if what is valuable is not transmuted and sublimated, and so made suitable for inclusion in the unified religion for the whole world. How are the theologians of Islam likely to respond to this challenge?

Bibliography

Charles C. Adams, *Islam and Modernism in Egypt*, London, 1933, an important study centred on the work of Muḥammad ʿAbduh.

Wilfred C. Smith, *Modern Islam in India*, London,

1946, etc.; the main interest is political, but some attention is paid to theology.

Sir Hamilton GIBB, *Modern Trends in Islam*, Chicago, 1947; an authoritative exposition of social and intellectual movements against their cultural background.

Appendix

NOTES

Abbreviations

EI[1], *EI*[2]: *Encyclopaedia of Islam*, first and second Editions.

EI(S): *Shorter Encyclopaedia of Islam*: see p. xxiii.

GAL, *GALS*, *GCAL*: see p. x.

Gardet and Anawati: *Introduction à la Théologie Musulmane*, see p. xx.

Massignon, *Passion*: see p. xix.

Massignon, *Essai*: see p. xix.

Montgomery Watt, *Free Will and Predestination*: see p. xxii.

Montgomery Watt, *Integration*: see p. xxii.

Montgomery Watt, "Political Attitudes": see p. 71.

Walzer, "Islamic Philosophy": see p. xxi.

Note on the Sources

Page xiii, 1. But cf. *Oriens*, vii. 204.

xiii, 2. Cf. I. Goldziher, *Vorlesungen*, 188, 352; and H. Ritter, in *Der Islam*, xviii (1929), 46 f.

xv, 3. Cf. Montgomery Watt, *Free Will and Predestination*, 48 f.; "Political Attitudes".

xv, 4. For the general point about biographies cf. H. A. R. Gibb, "Islamic Biographical Literature" in *Arabic, Persian and Turkish Historiography*, London, 1962.

xvi, 5. Paris, 1842–7, four vols. The title is *Wafayāt al-Aʿyān* or *The Obituaries of Eminent Men.*

xvi, 6. *Murūj adh-Dhahab* ("*Les Prairies d'Or*"),

edited and translated by C. Barbier de Meynard and Pavet de Courteille, Paris, 1861–77, nine vols.

xix, 7. A useful introduction is *Sufism*, by A. J. Arberry (London, 1950); there is a good bibliography in his *Introduction to the History of Sufism* (London, 1943). Another important work is *The Idea of Personality in Sufism*, by R. A. Nicholson (Cambridge, 1923).

xxi, 8. Munich, 1923. Florence, 1939; Paris, 1947.

Part One: THE UMAYYAD PERIOD

The Khārijites

Page 12, 1. The Arabic words are: *lā ḥukm illā li-'llāh.* Cf. Qur'ān, 6.57, etc.; also *Der Islam*, xxxvi. 217.

The Murji'ites and other Moderates

Page 28, 2. The sort of results that are possible may be gauged from ch. 3 (pp. 71-122) of C. Pellat's *Le Milieu baṣrien et la formation de Gaḥiẓ*, Paris, 1953, and also from the works in Arabic of Aḥmad Amīn.

30, 3. Translated by A. Guillaume, London, 1955.

34, 4. Cf. Wensinck, *Muslim Creed*, 22-4, 33, 37, etc.

Part Two: THE FIRST WAVE OF HELLENISM

Historical Background

Page 38, 1. Cf. Schacht, *Origins of Muhammadan Jurisprudence*, 95, 102 f. Also *GALS*, i. 236.

38, 2. It is not extant, but a Muslim refutation of it has been edited and translated into Italian by M. Guidi as *La lotta tra l'Islam e il manicheismo* (Rome, 1927). The review by H. S. Nyberg in *Orientalische Literatur-Zeitung*, xxxii (1929), 425-

441, is important. Cf. Montgomery Watt, *Integration*, 120 f.

THE TRANSLATORS AND THE FIRST PHILOSOPHERS

Page 45, 3. R. Walzer, "Islamic Philosophy", p. 133.
46, 4. *Rasā'il al-Kindī al-Falsafiyya*, Cairo, 1950, 104, 261.

THE EXPANSION OF SHĪ'ISM

Page 54, 5. Cf. L. Massignon, *Passion*, i. 140-51.
54, 6. *Maqālāt*, i. 64.

THE MU'TAZILITES

Page 59, 7. Cf. Montgomery Watt, *Free Will and Predestination*, 104-6; for the *Fihrist*, cf. *Zeitschrift der deutschen morgenländischen Gesellschaft*, xc (1936), 315, 317 (Fück) and *I.R.A. Miscellany*, I (1948), London, 1949, 33 (Arberry); cf. L. Massignon, *Essai*,[2] 167.
61, 8. In art. "Mu'tazila" in *EI*[1] and elsewhere.
61, 9. Montgomery Watt, "Political Attitudes".
65, 10. Notably C. H. Becker, "Christliche Polemik und islamische Dogmenbilding", in *Zeitschrift für Assyriologie*, xxvi (1911), 175-95, reprinted in *Islamstudien*, Leipzig, 1924, i. 432-49. There is is also an English translation. Cf. H. A. Wolfson, "The Muslim Attributes and the Christian Trinity", *Harvard Theological Review*, xlix (1949), 1-18; also in *JAOS*, lxxix (1959), 73-80.
69, 11. Cf. R. Paret, "An-Naẓẓām als Experimentator", *Der Islam*, xxv (1937), 228-33.
69, 12. See p. 86 below.

THE CONSOLIDATION OF SUNNISM

Page 73, 13. Cf. Montgomery Watt, "The Condemnation of the Jews of Banū Qurayẓah", *Muslim*

World, xlii (1952), 160-71; "The Materials used by Ibn Isḥaq" in *Arabic, Persian and Turkish Historiography*, London, 1962.

79, 14. Cf. Massignon, *Essai*,[2] 260-72, 318 f. Also C. E. Bosworth, "The Rise of the Karāmiyyah in Khurasan", *Muslim World*, l (1960), 5-14. A Ḥanafite, Muḥammad ibn-al-Yamān as-Samarqandī, perhaps connected with al-Māturīdī, wrote a refutation of the Karrāmites (*Al-Jawāhir al-Muḍī'a*, ii. 144, etc.). There is some dispute as to whether the name is as given or "Karām" or "Kirām".

80, 15. Something similar had been asserted earlier by Mālik ibn-Anas (d. 795); cf. ash-Shahrastānī, *Milal*, 65 (i. 125); etc.

81, 16. Cf. I. Goldziher, "Die dogmatische Partei der Sālimijja", *Zeitschrift der deutschen morgenländischen Gesellschaft*, lxi (1907), 73-80; L. Massignon, art. "Sālimīya" in *EI*[1], and *Essai*,[2] 294-300.

Al-Ash'arī

Page 87, 17. Cf. W. Montgomery Watt, "The Origin of the Islamic Doctrine of Acquisition", *Journal of the Royal Asiatic Society*, 1943, 234-47; the treatment of al-Ash'arī above is based on the section about him in *Free Will and Predestination in Early Islam* (see p. xxii above).

Part Three: THE SECOND WAVE OF HELLENISM

The Flowering of Philosophy

Page 93, 1. An account of the coterie's discussion of the death of the Buwayhid prince 'Aḍud-ad-

Dawla in March 983 is quoted from Abū-Ḥayyān in a history translated by H. F. Amedroz and D. S. Margoliouth, *The Eclipse of the 'Abbāsid Caliphate* (Oxford, 1920, etc.), vi. 76-8.

93, 2. See previous note.

94, 3. *Al-Fawz al-Asghar* is translated by J. W. Sweetman in *Islam and Christian Theology* (London, 1945), 1/i, 93-185.

94, 4. *Tahdhīb al-Akhlāq*: an English translation is promised. Further details of this and other ethical works in D. M. Donaldson, *A Study of Muslim Ethics*, London, 1953.

98, 5. R. Walzer in *Philosophies, Eastern and Western*, ii. 143.

The Vicissitudes of Shī'ism

Page 99, 6. Cf. *GALS*, i. 320-23, 704-14; etc.

99, 7. *A Shī'ite Creed*, translated by A. A. A. Fyzee, London, 1942.

99, 8. See p. 168 below.

100, 9. R. Strothmann, art. "al-Zaidīya" in *EI*[1], and other works. M. Guidi, *La lotta tra l'Islam e il manicheismo*, Rome, 1927 (translation of a Zaydite-Mu'tazilite text); also *Gli scrittori zayditi e l' esegesi coranica mu' tazilita*, Rome, 1925.

102, 10. A. J. Arberry in *Avicenna: Scientist and Philosopher* (ed. G. Wickens), 12. A different picture is given in *Kitāb Jāmi' al-Ḥikmatayn* ("Harmonie de la philosophie grecque et de la théosophie ismaélienne") by Nāṣir-i-Khusraw, composed 1069, edited by H. Corbin and M. Mo'in, Teheran, 1953; cf. the description in Arberry, *Reason and Revelation in Islam*, London, 1957, 72-82. (This work has other references to recently published texts.)

103, 11. By W. Ivanow, Bombay, 1936; the creed is *Tāj al-ʿAqāʾid* by Ibn-al-Walīd (*GALS*, ii. 715).
104, 12. Cf. Montgomery Watt, *Integration*, 67-78.
105, 13. For further information consult *EI(S)*, arts. "Druses", "Nuṣairī", "Mutawālī", "Yazīdī'", etc.

The Progress of Sunnite Theology

Page 107, 14. The part of the *Iʿjāz* dealing with poetry is translated (with notes) by G. E. von Grunebaum as *A Tenth-Century Document of Arab Literary Theory and Criticism* (Chicago, 1950). The other work, the *Bayān*, has been edited with an English summary by R. J. McCarthy as *Miracle and Magic*, Beirut, 1958.
112, 15. A shorter credal work is also translated in *Das Dogma des Imâm al-Ḥaramain al-Djuwainî und sein Werk al-ʿAqīdat an-Niẓâmîyah*, by H. Klopfer, Cairo/Wiesbaden, 1958.

Al-Ghazālī

Page 114, 16. For a preliminary survey see Margaret Smith, *Al-Ghazālī the Mystic*, ch. 13.
116, 17. Cf. F. Jabre, "La Biographie et l'œuvre de Ghazali reconsidérées . . .", *Mélanges de l'Institut Dominicain d'Études Orientales du Caire*, 1954, 73-102; M. Bouyges, *Essai de chronologie des œuvres de al-Ghazali*, Beirut, 1959.
117, 18. A possible exception is al-Abharī (d. 1265), but little is known about him; cf. *EI*², *GAL*, i. 608; *GALS*, i. 839. He wrote books on philosophy, which must have been favourite textbooks, since they were much commented on. This suggests that they were compendia rather than original works,

and that they were adapted to the needs of theologians.

Sunnite Theology from 1100 to 1250

Page 127, 19. Cf. Ritter in *Der Islam*, xviii (1929), 48-50.

129, 20. The interpretations of this tradition are discussed in W. Montgomery Watt, "Created in his Image", *Transactions of the Glasgow University Oriental Society*, xviii (1961), 38-49.

129, 21. Translated by D. B. Macdonald, *Development*, 308-15.

130, 22. George Makdisi, "Nouveaux Détails sur l'affaire d'ibn 'Aqīl", *Mélanges Louis Massignon*, Damascus, 1957, 91-126; cf. *Bulletin of the School of Oriental and African Studies*, xviii (1956), 9-31, 239-60; xix (1957), 13-48, 281-303, 426-43.

Part Four: THE PERIOD OF DARKNESS

The Sclerosis of Philosophical Theology

Page 151, 1. Montgomery Watt, *Integration*, 238-51.

153, 2. *EI²*, art. "al-Bayḍāwī"; Gardet and Anawati, 164 f.

153, 3. *EI(S)* art. "al-Nasafī (3)". He was interested in philosophy since he wrote a book called *Mi'yār an-Naẓar*, presumably about epistemology.

154, 4. *EI¹*, art. "al-Taftazānī"; Gardet and Anawati, 165-9.

154, 5. Cf. the Introduction of E. E. Elder's translation, *A Commentary on the Creed of Islam*, New York, 1950.

155, 6. Cf. *EI(S)*. art. "al-Sanūsī, Abū 'Abdallāh . . ."

156, 7. Translated into French by Garcin de Tassy, in *Exposition de la foi musulmane*, Paris, 1822.

156, 8. *La Djaouhara*, ed. and tr. with commentaries, by J. D. Luciani, Algiers, 1907.

157, 9. Art. "al-Bādjūrī" in *EI*[2].

The Vitality of the Ḥanbalites

Page 159, 10. Besides what he says in his *Essai sur Ibn Taimīya*, Laoust has written about the main Ḥanbalite doctors in "Le Hanbalisme sous le califat de Bagdad", *Revue des Études Islamiques*, 1959, 67-128.

The Transformation of Shī'ism

Page 169, 11. Cf. Laoust, *Essai sur Ibn Taimīya*, 36 f.

170, 12. *GALS*, ii. 577, 590.

170, 13. E. G. Browne, *Literary History of Persia*, iv. 410, etc.; *GALS*, ii. 844; Cl. Huart, art. "Shaikhī" in *EI*[1]. The Imāmite interest in Avicenna at this period is discussed by H. Corbin, *Avicenna and the Visionary Recital*, 243-57.

171, 14. Further references will be found in the articles by A. Bausani in *EI*[2], "Bābīs", "Bahā' Allāh", "Bahā'īs".

INDEX

(The Arabic article *al-*, with its variants such as *an-*, *ash-*, etc. is neglected in the alphabetical arrangement, except in the case of the word *Allāh*.)